Devotions
from Everyday Jobs

Devotions
from Everyday Jobs

by

Tammy Chandler

WordCrafts

Devotions from Everyday Jobs
Copyright 2017
Tammy Chandler

Author Photo by Portrait Innovations, Murfreesboro, Tennessee
Cover Design by David Warren

Scriptures quotations marked HCSB are taken from the Holman Christian Standard Bible Copyright 1999, 2000, 2002, 2003, 2009 by Holman Bible Publishers. Used by permission. Holman Christian Standard Bible, Holman CSB, and HCSB are federally registered trademarks of Holman Bible Publishers.

Scripture quotations marked (ESV) are from the Holy Bible, English Standard Version (ESV), copyright 2001 by Crossway, a publishing ministry of Good News Publishers. Used by permission. All rights reserved.

Scripture quotations marked NKJV are taken from the New King James Version. Copyright 1982 by Thomas Nelson, Inc. Used by permission. All rights reserved.

Scripture quotations marked KJV are taken from the Authorized Version, commonly referred to as the King James Version; public domain.

All rights reserved. No part of this book may be reproduced, stored in a retrieval system, or transmitted in any form or by any means—electronic, mechanical, photocopy, recording, or otherwise—without the prior written permission of the publisher. The only exception is brief quotations for review purposes.

Published by WordCrafts Press
Buffalo, Wyoming 82834
www.wordcrafts.net

For our children, Jonathan, Jordan and Charity, who have shown me the world of possibilities around us each and every day. I am blessed beyond belief to have you call me "Mom."

Love you forever and always.

Contents

Foreword i

Preface ii

Acknowledgements iv

The Farmer 1

The Dental Hygienist 4

The Lawyer 7

The Emergency Medical Technician 10

The Accountant 13

The Author 16

The Substitute Teacher 19

The Bank Teller 22

The General Contractor 25

The Law Enforcement Officer 28

The Tea Shop Owner 31

The Bus Driver 34

The Dry Cleaner 37

The Tour Guide 40

The Grandparent 43

The Dump Truck Driver 46

The Electrician 49

The Emergency Room Nurse 52

The Engineer 55

The Tow Truck Driver 58

The Event Planner ... 61
The Firefighter ... 64
The Florist ... 67
The Funeral Director ... 70
The Travel Agent ... 73
The Graffiti Artist ... 76
The Hair Stylist ... 79
The Usher ... 82
The Kindergarten Teacher ... 85
The Landscaper ... 88
The Locksmith ... 91
The Make Up Artist ... 94
The Mechanic ... 97
The Body Builder ... 100
The Meter Reader ... 103
The Middle School Teacher ... 106
The Mover ... 109
The Musician ... 112
The Nutritionist ... 115
The Optician ... 118
The Painter ... 121
The Pediatrician ... 124
The Pedicurist ... 127
The Photographer ... 130

The Pilot 133

The Plumber 136

The Postal Worker 139

The Preschool Teacher 142

The Professional Organizer 145

The Publisher 148

The Recycler 151

The Salesman 154

The Wood Cutter 157

The Sanitation Worker 160

The Server 163

The Soldier 166

The Song Writer 169

The Veteran 172

The Weather Forecaster 175

The Staffing Personnel 178

Foreword

When I was in the second grade, I had a great decision to make—would I be a nurse or a schoolteacher. When I found out nurses give needles and must clean up after sick people—admirable qualities to be sure, but not part of my makeup, I chose teaching. There are not many people who make their career choices in the second grade. Some of us have had many different jobs through the years. Some of us have expanded our areas of expertise, and some have changed careers midstream. Many of us have fallen into the jobs we currently work, and sometimes, we are discouraged. Does this job have any meaning, any purpose, in light of eternity? Do I make a difference, or just a paycheck?

God created every detail of your life and mine. Every job, every career, every step is part of His plan. And when we look at our work through the eyes of Creator God, it is good. As we punch the clock, we experience His calling. As we work, we find His purpose. As we succeed, we give Him glory. *Devotions from Everyday Jobs* is an opportunity to see our work as more—to see the callings He has placed in our lives through it, and to enjoy those callings. I am humbled and grateful that He gave me the eyes to see our work in this light, and has allowed me to share these blessings with you. I look forward to this journey with you and I am praying for you.

Enjoy your calling.

Preface

Devotions from Everyday Jobs is the fourth book of the *Devotions from Everyday Things* series. Each book in the series is a devotional in which you will find spiritual truths connected with ordinary things. It's a straightforward approach toward helping us on our journey to find deeper spiritual truths in the work around us; a journey to open our eyes to the calling of God in the work we do.

How to use this book: The devotions are uncomplicated, quiet times with God. Each one contains a daily Scripture passage, an illustration connected to a particular job, a Thought-provoker, and a Prayer Starter. The Scripture passage allows us to see where the connection to God's Word is; the illustration will help us apply the principles of Scripture to something we can take with us throughout the day. The Thought-provoker is an opportunity to adjust our thinking or actions to the principles learned from the devotion; it is also a Journal prompt if you prefer to write your thoughts. The prayer is a conversation starter about the topic of the devotion. It is an opportunity for us to thank God for what we are learning, and to ask Him for the strength we need to apply new Biblical principles to our hearts and lives. It is also a time for us to share our burdens and pour out our hearts about personal struggles we are facing.

You can also join me at my blog site:

www.simplydevotions.wordpress.com

You will find encouragement, updates and more postings to help keep us all going in this adventure into deeper spiritual truths. It's time to be excited about being a Christian—we can enjoy the work we do as we see the One who has called us to it.

Thank you for joining me for this journey through our callings in **_Devotions from Everyday Jobs_**. I am humbled, and so excited you have chosen this book, and I am praying for us to know God in a deeper, richer way because of this journey. Let's get started.

Acknowledgements

A dream takes a team, and while I am amazed that we are on the fourth book of *The Devotions from Everyday Things* series, there are those who have believed in this dream without wavering.

To my family, who continue to encourage me to write and allow me to tell our stories, for your support, suggestions and laughter at those times when I need it most, thank you.

To my Lighthouse church family, thank you for your support and for allowing me to share your lives in my writings. You are the prayer support and the exhorters I need in those moments of spiritual battle. Thank you.

To my friends, who put up with my crazy schedule and love me anyway—love you to the ends of the earth. To Kathy, who keeps me talking and then nudges me to keep writing so you have something new to read—you are the best.

To Mike and Paula Parker and the team at WordCrafts Press—only eternity will show the true investment you have made in the lives of the writers you touch. You go beyond the duties of publishers and you lovingly reach into our lives and bring out the creative potential we each have. Thank you for trusting me through this process each time and giving the freedom and the guidance to put words onto the page.

And most of all, to Him who is able to do more than we can ask or imagine, to Him, be the glory!

Devotions from Everyday Jobs

The Farmer

"The hardworking farmer must be first to partake of the crops. Consider what I say, and may the Lord give you understanding in all things."

2 Timothy 2:6 NKJV

Some may think the farmer is an obvious choice for a devotional book about everyday jobs. After all, Scripture abounds with images of throwing seed, reaping harvests, pulling out weeds and watching the fields. While all of those are important aspects of his job, the farmer I am referring today is the modern one. He doesn't use a mule team and a sickle to harvest his fields—he uses a hay cutter or a combine to do hundreds of acres in a short period of time. Fields are planted in one day using modern equipment and computer analysis is used to determine watershed, erosion, plant production and even profits.

Modern farmers know much about fertilizers, mineral depletion in soils, rain cycles, frost lines and bottom lines. To limit farmers to old ideas about seeding and harvesting is to limit the increase of their crops and the scope of their imaginations.

We have a farmer friend who tells us that he is always dreaming up new ways to improve farming. The principles of seeding and harvesting do not change—you plant seed, you get plants; you harvest plants, you get food. Farmers know this to be true, and the images of Scripture cement the concepts that God created the laws of sowing and harvesting. He did not, however, tell us that we had to use the same methods they did in 2000 BC to harvest crops. And He does not say anywhere that the methods of discipleship were set in stone either. He didn't limit us in the ways we can reach people—the only limitation is that we reach them with the same message of redemption He gave in His Word, through His Son, the day He split history in two.

So, as we start this journey into the world of everyday work, please do not limit yourself to old methods—labels of certain jobs as blue- or white-collar, pay scales or salaries, hands-on or office types. We are each called to reach others with the same message—the good news of the Gospel—but the methods God gives each of us to do that will be different, and they are all good. Let's see our work as more than just an everyday job. Let's see our work as God does—He's given us each a calling. Let's answer that call with all the imagination and insight He can give as we make an impact on the kingdom of God with our everyday jobs. Let's get started!

Thought-provoker:

What do we think about jobs? Are we allowing old ideas to limit our reach? How can we open our minds to new methods while staying true to the original message of the Gospel?

Father, as we start this journey through our everyday work, help us to see You, to see the calling You have placed on each one of our lives. In Jesus' name, Amen.

Notes/Insights:

The Dental Hygienist

> "Not by works of righteousness which we have done, but according to His mercy He saved us, through the washing of regeneration and renewing of the Holy Spirit, whom He poured out on us abundantly through Jesus Christ our Savior, that having been justified by His grace we should become heirs according to the hope of eternal life. This is a faithful saying, and these things I want you to affirm constantly, that those who have believed in God should be careful to maintain good works. These things are good and profitable to men."
>
> Titus 3:5-8 NKJV

I have a friend who is a dental hygienist. She is a fun loving, smiling individual who loves her job and is very good at what she does. When asked what she does for a living, she says, "I'm a scum scraper." Not exactly a pretty picture of her career, but accurate nonetheless. Her job requires that she scrape the scum—the tartar and buildup—off the teeth of her clients. She does this to help them remain healthy and have a vibrant smile.

No matter how hard I try, no matter what products I use, I cannot get the tartar off my teeth myself. Oh, I can use strong fluoride toothpaste, and I can rinse, gargle and floss each day, but I cannot get the tartar off. I must go see my friend for that, and she is glad to do it, knowing that her ability to "scrape scum" makes my life and health better.

Jesus Christ is the scum-scraper of sin. He took the penalty on the cross and He bore our sins so that we could be spiritually healthy and free to smile. He gives us the joy to be able to shine a bright light in a dark world. We cannot do it without Him. There are many who try—they pile on the fluoride of good works or the flossing of generosity, but those things do not save them from the scum of sin. Only Jesus can do that.

When my hygienist friend finishes with a client, she hands them the new toothbrush and reminds them that even though they cannot get the scum off their teeth alone, they still should mind good brushing and flossing habits and stay away from too much sugar or acid in their diets. Those things have nothing to do with removing the tartar, but they do create an environment where tartar does not have so much influence on their health. Our passage today reminds us that good works are not about saving us, but they are profitable, after we have been saved, to show others the way to a relationship with God. Jesus scrapes the scum of sin from our lives with His forgiveness and we, in turn, show our smiles to the world so they can see what He has done.

Thought-provoker:

Are we trying to scrape the sin scum off with our own works or are we trusting Christ alone for our salvation? Are we living in good works so others see the good work of God in us?

Lord, thank You for all You did to save us from sin. Help us to live so others see how profitable a life with You really is. In Jesus' name, Amen.

Notes/Insights:

The Lawyer

"My little children, I am writing you these things so that you may not sin. But if anyone does sin, we have an advocate with the Father—Jesus Christ the Righteous One. He Himself is the propitiation for our sins, and not only for ours, but also for those of the whole world."

1 John 2:1-2 HCSB

Lawyers are in a unique position. They are asked to step into circumstances where two parties are polarized, where emotions can be volatile, and they are asked to represent the facts. Whether it is a corporate negotiation or an inheritance dispute, lawyers must advocate for their clients. They are to publicly support their clients and their causes. For inheritance attorneys, they must abide by the will of the person who passed away and make sure the final wishes are carried out among family members. If no will is present, the attorney then must research family history, personal writings and any other information that helps to determine who has a right to property and possessions.

For corporate lawyers, they are required to support the causes of their clients, whether it is making sure expansions follow the law to avoid fines and penalties, or it is the buyout of another company and making sure assets and futures are protected on both sides.

For an adoption lawyer, he/she supports the parents in adding a child legally to their family and the child's advocate makes sure the family will love and provide for the child, as a family should.

Our passage today says that Jesus is our Advocate with the Father. He is our lawyer who represents the facts and supports us. He supports us—the sinners we are, and despite the things we have done, He supports us. When He goes before the Holy Judge, the Father, He supports us. He brings the facts—He went to the cross in our place and though we are thoroughly guilty, He paid the price. His blood and His scars were for us. He put Himself in our place so we could join Him in heavenly places (Ephesians 1).

He chooses to continue to support us and to represent us before the heavenly court. Each time we sin, He goes before the Father and presents His sacrifice as our fine and His blood as our penalty. He took our place and He supports us. How much more of a reason do we need to stop intentionally sinning? The facts and evidence of His grace and mercy should be more than enough to overcome temptations, but when it is not, He is our heavenly lawyer. He supports us.

Thought-provoker:
Are we living in the facts and evidence of Jesus' great love and mercy or are we selfishly living in the shadows of sin?

Father, thank You for the heavenly Advocate we have in Jesus. Help us to live in light of the evidence of Your great love and mercy and forsake the shadows of sin as we learn just how much it cost You to support us. When we do sin, help us to be quick to repent and lean into our Advocate. In Jesus' name, Amen.

Notes/Insights:

The Emergency Medical Technician

"Do not have other gods besides Me."
Exodus 20:3 HCSB

Emergency Medical Technicians have very important jobs. They are the first responders to medical emergencies, and their focus must be on the most critical injury. When they arrive on a scene, there may be cuts and bruises, but they must see past that to the broken bones, internal injuries, or head injuries which are much more serious, but cannot be seen immediately. EMTs know the questions to ask to determine what injuries are more threatening, which ones are minor and which ones need urgent care. The EMT discovers the injuries and then he/she passes the patient to the skilled hands of doctors who specialize in those injuries.

In life, there are many issues that present themselves as urgent. There are the scrapes and bruises of hurt feelings, long lists of tasks that need to be done, or minor interruptions to our plans; and then there are the urgent things that are much, much deeper, but harder to see.

We put Band-Aids on the feelings, but don't get to the root issues that are causing them. If an EMT put a Band-Aid on the forehead of a concussion victim that EMT would be removed from his/her position immediately by supervisors. The EMT must have the wisdom to know the difference between a superficial symptom and a root cause. We would do well to learn the same.

Many times, the immediate symptoms that show up in our hearts are not the ones that we need to treat. We have deeper issues of idols—anything that comes between us and God—and the Bible spells out what those things can be. As an example, Colossians 3:5 tells us that sexual immorality, any kind of impurity, wrong passions, evil desires and covetousness are all heart idols. These heart issues must be dealt with strongly, deeply and thoroughly by the work of God in our hearts.

Band-Aids don't cut it when we are dealing with selfish desires and misdirected passions. We are the EMTs—we recognize the deep issues in our hearts and then we must take them to God and allow Him to work as the Great Physician. We must be willing to do more than a bandage—we must allow Him to cut away the idols in our hearts and to replace them with the healing that comes only by putting Him first. But, He will not do that unless we are first willing to bring them to Him.

The EMTs bring the injured to the doctor; we need to bring our heart idols to the Lord. That is when true healing begins, and the EMTs know they did their job well—when the patient survives and the real issues are treated.

Thought-provoker:
Are you bringing the true heart issues and idols to the Great Physician in your life today, or are you just putting on a bandage and pretending everything is okay?

Father, thank You for the example of the EMTs who bring the real issues to light so doctors can treat them. Help us bring our heart issues to You for healing today, because temporary bandages aren't helping. In Jesus' name, Amen.

Notes/Insights:

The Accountant

"A good man produces good things from his storeroom of good, and an evil man produces evil things from his storeroom of evil. I tell you that on the day of judgment people will have to account for every careless word they speak."

Matthew 12:35-36 HCSB

Two of my brothers-in-law are accountants and I am fascinated with how their minds work. When others see a shopping trip, they see an expense account; where there is a debt, they see a payoff. They have the amazing ability to be able to do math —real math problems—in their heads without breaking a sweat. They understand tax codes, logistics and finance vocabulary I have never heard. Our son has decided to study accounting in college as well and he brings home very interesting problems. Compound interest, expense accounting and reconciling sheet problems that take pages to complete—and he enjoys tackling them.

The reconciling sheets interest me. Every detail of expenditures for a particular company is captured on those sheets. Hundreds of employees, various expense accounts and company credit card statements are all brought together in one report. Every receipt is recorded and every category is added up until all the expenses of the company are accounted and known. The report is passed to the leadership of the company, and eventually reported to the government, to keep the company accountable to do things correctly and legally. Without the accountants, individuals could steal money from the company and no one would ever know, or the company could be sitting on a cash flow and have no idea. For good or bad, the accountant records all the transactions of the company so everyone knows where it stands.

All our words and deeds are being recorded and someday, the sheets will be reconciled. Good or evil, intentional or careless, we are making an accounting report with our lives. We will stand one day and give an account (1 Corinthians 3). The good we have done for the kingdom will survive; the rest will burn up. This would seem so unfair, except we know the day of accounting is coming, and we have the ability to be intentional about our words and deeds. When we understand that Christ paid our debt, a debt so huge we could never have begun to pay it back, then keeping track of our words and deeds should not be a great effort. We need to refrain from saying those angry words and doing something evil, and instead we need to be intentional about our kindness, humility and gentleness. Add those things to our personal accounting and leave the hurtful, evil careless things off our balances.

When we remember the reconciling Christ has already done for us, we can do the math, and be kind.

Thought-provoker:
How well are we reconciling our words and deeds when it comes to our Christian walk?

Abba, thank You that we know we will give an account and help us to be intentional in our kindness and humility today and everyday. In Jesus' name, Amen.

Notes/Insights:

The Author

> "Likewise the Spirit also helps in our weaknesses. For we do not know what we should pray for as we ought, but the Spirit Himself makes intercession for us with groanings which cannot be uttered."
> Romans 8:26 NKJV

This should be an easy one for me to write. After all, I have written previous works, I know the process, and I enjoy putting words together on paper. Ideas flow in and out of my mind as I work, relax and even when I try to sleep. I keep notepads by my bed, on my desk and around the house so I can jot down words or phrases. I keep a pen and paper in my purse all the time because one never knows when an idea will flutter into thought and turn into an idea. And yet, when it comes to putting down on paper the job that I do…

Maybe the reason it is so difficult to relate this particular job is because the origin of ideas is not my own. What I mean is that the Spirit of God must plant the seed of connection between a spiritual truth and an everyday object for me to have anything to say. In the process of daily living, I study the Bible. I try to be a diligent student (2 Timothy 2:15) and then the Holy Spirit will nudge me in a direction of study. He will show me a verse, or verses in the study, that clarify truth or teach me a principle. As I go through my day, I try to find an illustration of the truth I have learned and try to connect it to something tangible that helps me remember. Then, I must write something down. Sometimes, only a word comes to mind, or a phrase, or an idea. If that illustration fits with the Scripture, then I have a devotion idea.

At times, though, nothing seems to fit. I cannot put two words together, let alone an entire idea. But that does not mean the Spirit isn't teaching me, it just means I have not caught on as the student. The Spirit is still at work teaching me, guiding me, showing me principles and truths—I just have not grasped them because of the weakness of my flesh or the hindrance of a wrong attitude. As He continues to work, I continue to learn.

I am so grateful that He does not give up. Even when I do not know what to write, He has a plan. When I do not know what to pray, He has the words. When I have failed, He is faithful. When I am rebellious, He is still righteous. And when I am willing, He gives me something to say. I guess writing about what I do wasn't so difficult after all. My heavenly Father already knew what to say.

Thought-provoker:

Are we consistently learning truth, or are we avoiding the process?

Lord, thank You for Your leading and teaching in our lives. Help us to receive Your truth and remember what we have learned. In Jesus' name, Amen.

Notes/Insights:

The Substitute Teacher

"But a hireling, he who is not the shepherd, one who does not own the sheep, sees the wolf coming and leaves the sheep and flees; and the wolf catches the sheep and scatters them."

John 10:12 NKJV

I have great respect for substitute teachers—I was one. It takes confidence, and sometimes a lot of courage, to walk into another teacher's classroom and attempt to keep order and encourage learning for one day. I also know that substitute teachers care about the students, and especially the teacher who is out sick or needing the day to attend to some other matter. The substitute, however, is at a distinct disadvantage—she does not know the students.

One of the experiences I had as a substitute has stayed with me. The class realized they were having a substitute and before I could get the role taken and everyone seated, several students got up and left. There was nothing I could do about it because I did not know who the students were and I had no way of chasing them down without leaving the few students who remained unattended. I took role, went through the lesson plans and gave the remaining students an easy assignment as a reward for staying. I left a note detailing the experience for the regular teacher, and then I left. I had no more responsibilities, no more connection, and no contact, with that class. It was just one day.

False teachers are substitute teachers, but unlike most substitute teachers, they have no care for the souls in the classroom of life. The regular teacher is still present—God is always available to teach us the ways in which we should go, but these false teachers who deny God's Word, deter students from class. They have no concern for the plans and designs the teacher has and they do not even care if the students learn anything the regular teacher has planned. They come in temporarily and wreak havoc. They are the worst type of substitutes—their agenda is to cause distraction and despair. They do not care if students leave before the lesson starts and they prefer the students sever connections with their true teacher.

God, as the Master Teacher, warned us about these substitutes. He told us the truth—they are not good shepherds. He told us to be careful, because these false teachers will allow the wolf (a picture of the devil) to enter the flock and scatter the sheep. We must be sure the teachers we attend to, listen to and connect with are sound teachers of The Word. In this case, do not accept substitutes.

Thought-provoker:

Are we listening to the Master Teacher or are we accepting substitutes? Are we being true teachers who honor the Master Teacher?

Lord, thank You for being the Master Teacher who shares truth with us and for giving us those who truly desire to teach us Your ways. Help us not to listen to false substitutes, but to know the truth and hold to it. In Jesus' name, Amen.

Notes/Insights:

The Bank Teller

> "Love is patient and kind. Love is not jealous or boastful or proud or rude. It does not demand its own way. It is not irritable, and it keeps no record of being wronged."
>
> I Corinthians 13:4-5 NLT

I have a confession—I really enjoy going to the bank. The ladies and gentlemen who work there are very friendly and helpful. It sounds cliché, I know, but the bank tellers where I keep my account are the very embodiment of customer service and core company values. They know me on a first name basis, they know about our children's activities and plans and they ask about the good things happening in our lives while I am doing my banking.

They have also been there when things have not been so good, and they are especially kind when I make a mistake—in my adding. You see, my sons and husband are gifted with minds that can do numbers quickly and accurately. I am not blessed with that gift—I have to write down every number and a calculator is almost always a necessity for me to get all the digits added correctly. When I try to hurry through the numbers, I usually make a mistake.

Now, the bank teller's job is to keep accurate accounts—he/she makes sure the numbers add up. When they find my mistakes, they are very gracious to let me know. They do not chide me for my hurriedness and they do not berate my math skills. No matter how many times I make a mistake, they simply smile and say, "We caught this—you actually have more money than you thought in your deposit today. Is it okay if we adjust it?"

Love is like a Bank Teller. While it is love's job to keep accurate accounts of our lives—after all, parents who love their children discipline them (Hebrews 12), love does not keep records of the wrongs. It corrects them, like the Bank Tellers adjust accounting mistakes on my deposits, and then lets them go. The tellers do not tell me, "You've made too many addition mistakes this month, so we are going to have to penalize you." No, instead we all know that I tend to get distracted, so I bring a calculator and double check my math, and they check it again to be sure things are correct. And they still welcome me again, even after I made a mistake the last time. That's what love does.

Thought-provoker:

Are we loving like Bank Tellers and helping others correct mistakes without holding grudges, or are we counting up the mistakes to get to our selfish limits? What do we need to let go of today?

Father, thank You for Bank Tellers who are kind and patient. Help us to remember that this is what love looks like—it corrects the wrongs and then lets them go. Help us love like that today, and always. In Jesus' name, Amen.

Notes/Insights:

The General Contractor

"In My Father's house are many mansions; if it were not so, I would have told you. I go to prepare a place for you. And if I go and prepare a place for you, I will come again and receive you to Myself; that where I am, there you may be also."

John 14:2-3 NKJV

When we decided to renovate our house, we called several contractors. We interviewed them, and we decided to go with a particular gentleman because we appreciated his honesty and he told us the price of the project and that everything was included. He came and spent some time with us, but when the work started, it was the crew that came to the house each day. Don oversaw the project, but he was not present on the job site. If there was a problem, he was contacted and he made the final decisions about what needed to be done, but he did not have to come to job site for the work to get done. He was always close to the project, and he had the master blueprint for how it should be done.

Jesus is the General Contractor of our lives. Yes, there are other contractors out there who claim to be able to help us build a life of character, goodness, works, etc., but there is only one contractor, who knows how to build a Godly life, and He included everything we need in the price, and He paid it too. He came and started the project—He lived and died, then rose again to build the foundation. But then He went away. He sent the Holy Spirit to comfort and challenge us to grow into the renovations of a spiritual walk with Him, and even though Jesus is not physically present on earth, the work in our lives is still getting done. When we have questions, we can reach out and talk to Jesus through prayer and faith, and He makes the final decisions about the renovations in our lives. As long as we are willing, the changes do happen and the improvements are made.

There was a day that Don did come to the job site—the final inspection. He walked through each room, checked the craftsmanship and made sure we were happy with the final product. One day, and hopefully soon, Jesus will be coming back for His final inspection—He will call us home to the place He has prepared for us, and it will be beyond our wildest imaginations.

Thought-provoker:

Are we allowing Jesus to renovate our lives to be what He wants them to be? What do we need to allow the Holy Spirit to do in our hearts today?

Lord, thank You for having the master plan for our lives. Please make us willing to accept the renovations You have for us and to grow and change as You want. And even so come quickly! In Jesus' name, Amen.

Notes/Insights:

The Law Enforcement Officer

> "For he is God's minister to you for good. But if you do evil, be afraid; for he does not bear the sword in vain; for he is God's minister, an avenger to execute wrath on him who practices evil."
> Romans 13:4 NKJV

I am honored to know several Law Enforcement Officers. From friends at church, to family members, it is a privilege to put a face and personality to more than just a label. These individuals take their professions seriously and they know the life and death decisions that lie outside the door every time they sign up for another shift. They also realize that many, many people in the community have nothing but respect and good perceptions of the law enforcement profession.

Because of good community relations, and good consciences on both sides, there is no reason to fear a police officer, and the officers have mutual respect for the citizens they protect. When our children were younger, we took them to the police department and allowed them to meet officers and get to know their names. We explained to them that if they were ever hurt, lost, or needed help, the police officers were there as friends. The officers also explained to our children that they were there to keep others from hurting them and if someone ever did try to harm them, a police officer was another in the line of protection they could run to and be safe.

Safety—such a complex concept into today's difficult world. Yet, God designed law enforcement and order long before our nation existed. God knew the wicked imaginations of mankind would need law, and those who are willing to enforce it, to keep things decently and in order. Without the power of enforcement, law has no meaning. The lessons the officers taught our children when they were young, still apply today—even if we are older and taller. The officers are there to protect. Just as God protects His own, officers are enlisted in God's design to protect others. God allows human representations of protection so we can see the greater Protector He is and respond to His love for us.

Friendship—the only time to fear, according to today's text, is when we practice evil, when we violate the law. And then it is our responsibility to accept the consequences for the choices we made and the law we trespassed. Because I do my best to live with a clear conscience, I am not afraid of our law enforcement friends. We, in fact, support them in the work they do by praying for them, encouraging them and being proud of them for doing what God has called them to do.

Thought-provoker:

How do we perceive law enforcement officers? Knowing they are part of God's design, how can we encourage them today?

Father, thank You for those who stand on the front line of our protection and safety. Please watch over them and give them a good day in the work You have called them to do. Help us to live in such a way that we have nothing to fear from them. In Jesus' name, Amen.

Notes/Insights:

The Tea Shop Owner

"The heart of the wise teaches his mouth, and adds learning to his lips. Pleasant words are like a honeycomb, sweetness to the soul and health to the bones."

Proverbs 16:23-24 NKJV

I have a friend who owns a tea shop. Despite her busy life in ministry, she felt a God-given desire to be a tea specialist—one who has learned the art of blending ingredients to make teas to help others. God granted her desire and now she owns a tea shop and she blends amazing teas. Some of her teas are for specific conditions—she can blend a tea for sinus relief or to calm the nerves. Others are blended just for their taste and enjoyment.

She has taken her tea blends and integrated them into an amazing tea shop. She has comfy couches where people can come in, drop into a comfortable seat, add their headphones and just relax, or they can open their business caches and work on the day's paperwork. Friends visit at the small tables and converse in the peaceful atmosphere. But, my favorite invitation is when Sue asks someone to sit at the "bar." It's the place where people usually sit when they come in alone, and Sue makes them feel welcome. She stops what she is doing and spends time listening. She hears about struggles, or joys, and she blends humor with compassion to make things better.

Sue has learned the art of blending. She has mastered tea ingredients that go together, and she knows, sometimes, bitter elements have to be added to balance the tea's flavor.

If everything were sweet, the tea would leave a syrupy taste; too bitter, and the customer won't finish it. But, by blending the ingredients of sweet and bitter origins, she finds a tea that has full layers of flavor that customers savor. Sue knows that life is a blending as well.

As she listens to the different elements of a customer's situation, she discerns whether they need encouragement, a little exhortation, a dash of mercy or a heaping spoonful of humor. Her willingness to see others gives her the opportunity to speak a blend of godliness and love into their hearts. We need both. When life's situations become hard, we need some sweetness to remind us that God is still good. When we are being stubborn or refusing to accept God's calling, we need a little confrontation—bitterness—to remind us Whose we are and why we serve Him.

I am glad Sue has learned the art of blending, and I hope we will accept the ingredients of life God has for us, and see how He is making a master cup, full of many different flavors, that makes life worth the savoring. I know Sue does, and I think it's time for another cup of Sue's well-blended tea.

Thought-provoker:

Have we ever thought of how many different life-ingredients it takes to make a life worth savoring?

Lord, thank You that You are the Master who blends the ingredients of this life in a beautiful blend that we can savor. Thank You our lives are full of Your blend. In Jesus' name, Amen.

Notes/Insights:

The Bus Driver

> "Enter by the narrow gate; for wide is the gate and broad is the way that leads to destruction, and there are many who go in by it. Because narrow is the gate and difficult is the way which leads to life, and there are few who find it."
>
> Matthew 7:13-14 NKJV

The bus driver—the mention of it brings a rush of childhood memories for some as they remember their favorite elementary transport personnel. The person who smiled each morning at the bus stop and dropped each student off safely at the end of the day. Or, maybe an athlete remembers the guy who drove the bus for the team, and maybe still another person remembers the sweet lady who drove the transit bus in your college town. For some of us, the bus driver was a person with a name tag—a quiet individual who did their job and reached destinations, but rarely interacted with the passengers. Other drivers were lively and conversational—like the bus driver we had for a concert choir trip in college. He was interested in what we were studying, where we were going and he helped pass the travel time between stops with funny stories and lively conversation.

No matter their personalities, bus drivers ultimately have a very important job: they get people from where they are to where they want to go. Whether it is a school bus that follows the same route twice every day, or if it is a tour bus that goes to a different location each weekend, the bus will not go without a driver. The driver is the one who knows where to go and how to get there. In the case of our choir trip, I had no idea what route we would take, but Roy knew (and this was before the days of GPS). He knew the alternate routes as well as the fastest and most direct ones. He got us to our destinations on time and he even stuck around to enjoy our concert at one of the stops.

As spiritual leaders, we are bus drivers. Jesus tells us He is the Way (John 14:6) and we are to bring others to a relationship with Him as Savior and Lord (Acts 1:8). Sometimes, we can be very direct and get them to that destination quickly. These passengers are eager to hear the stories and want to reach their desired location quickly. Other times, it takes an alternate route, patience and a quiet demeanor to allow them to come close to the Savior. Regardless of how you are, drive the bus. Pick up others along the way and take them to the destination of an opportunity to meet Jesus, and I do not mean by scaring them half to death with your driving skills. Be like Roy. Interact, ask questions and make the journey pleasant. Give them an adventure as you show them your awesome Savior.

Thought-provoker:

Are we picking up others on our journey and allowing them to find the Savior?

Father, thank You for allowing us to participate in bringing others to You in this life journey. Help us to be good bus drivers who represent You well and bring others into the kingdom. In Jesus' name, Amen.

Notes/Insights:

The Dry Cleaner

"That He might sanctify and cleanse her with the washing of water by the word, that He might present her to Himself a glorious church, not having spot or wrinkle or any such thing, but that she should be holy and without blemish."

Ephesians 5:26-27 NKJV

I normally do not have to visit the dry cleaners because most of our clothes are cotton blended, goes-in-the-washer-type of clothes. There are a few pieces we own, however, that are "Dry Clean Only" because of their fabric or design and those pieces get a special trip to the Dry Cleaners. These clothes get extra special treatment because they are valuable. First, they were expensive to purchase. Second, they are valuable because they are uniforms or dresses that are only used for special occasions. Third, they are preserved. You won't find the dry clean only pieces of clothing rumpled on the floor or thrown in a corner. They are kept neatly in the closet. Fourth, they are worn with pride and confidence, and they symbolize the organizations to which our family members belong or the importance of the gathering being attended.

While our dry cleaner does not know us personally, he understands the importance of the clothes we bring to him and he treats them accordingly. He makes sure the jackets and pants are crisp and pressed, and the dresses are wrinkle free and pristine. He makes sure there are no stains or smells in the clothing and he double checks them before we leave his shop to be sure we will be satisfied with the results. If a button is missing, he fixes it. If a collar is bent, he represses it. He wants to make sure the clothing that leaves his store is a wonderful representation of his work, and he goes above and beyond to make sure it is.

The church is the "dry clean only" masterpiece of God. She was expensive to purchase—she cost Him his own life and blood on a cross. She is valuable to Him as He calls her His bride, the most cherished relationship known on earth. He preserves and protects her and gives her a place of honor and respect because she belongs to Him. He is proud of her and wants to show the world what His love looks like in her shining eyes and her beautiful garments of grace. We belong to the family of God, and as such, we should look like it. No stains of sin left uncovered by forgiveness; no wrinkles of worldliness marring our wardrobe as we shine in the glory of His love.

Thought-provoker:

Are we willing to be cleansed from our sin, not just at the moment of salvation, but daily as we live as the representation of God's very best?

Father, thank You for presenting us as a glorious testament of Your love and grace. Help us to be the holy and unblemished bride You have called us to be. And when we sin, help us to be quick to confess and forsake it and restore a right relationship with You. In Jesus' name, Amen.

Notes/Insights:

The Tour Guide

> "Thomas said to him, 'Lord, we do not know where you are going. How can we know the way?' Jesus said to him, 'I am the way, and the truth, and the life. No one comes to the Father except through me. If you had known me, you would have known my Father also. From now on you do know him and have seen him.'"
>
> John 14:5-7 ESV

My sister-in-law studied tourism in college. I thought it was an interesting major. While I love my sister-in-law and respect her choices, I could not help but think: What would you need to study for four years about showing others the sights around a famous town? So, I did a little research, and it is amazing how much professional tour guides actually have to know. They must decide where they want to work, and they need to spend time learning the customs and culture of the area. They then must learn the history of the area and the people who made that area famous. They must learn evacuation routes in case of emergencies, and they have to know the protocols for foreigners arriving and departing from their vacation destinations. The more I researched, the more I realized how much knowledge these tourism majors must learn in just four short years.

In our passage today, Thomas, and the other disciples, had been with Jesus for almost three years. He was preparing them to be the tour guides of the Gospel, and they were still lost. Not lost, meaning they didn't know Who Jesus was, but lost in the sense that they did not grasp the importance of what He was preparing them to do. They were still searching out other destinations in their minds, they had their own expectations of what the Messiah should be, and what Jesus was telling them was very different. Fortunately, they grasped the mission.

After Christ arose, the disciples led so many others to the Savior; they turned the world upside down (Acts 17:6). They learned the culture, the customs and the communities around them. They showed others the immense importance of The Way—Jesus—and they were able to clearly lead others to the eternal destination awaiting them in grace and through faith in Christ. We are in the tourism business too. We are to be leading others to the Gospel and allowing them to find their eternal destination in a relationship with Jesus Christ. And we do not have to study for four years to start—we just need to start pointing the way.

Thought-provokers:

Are we the tour guides leading others to life in Christ? Are we showing others the eternal destination awaiting them?

Lord, help us to be the tour guides that lead the world to You. Don't allow us to make excuses, help us to start doing it right now, here, where we are. In Jesus' name, Amen.

Notes/Insights:

The Grandparent

> "And thou shalt teach them diligently unto thy children, and shalt talk of them when thou sittest in thine house, and when thou walkest by the way, and when thou liest down, and when thou risest up."
>
> Deuteronomy 6:7 KJV

It has been said that grandparenting is the reward for surviving parenthood. It is a time when you get to enjoy children instead of having to rear them and be concerned about the outcome. Someone else has to do the hard work of potty training, manners and etiquette while grandparents engage in the fun side of family.

But for some, the job of grandparenting has become more than just fun. Some grandparents find themselves taking care of the second family generation, having to be part of the growing up process on more than just birthdays and holidays. Whether by choice or necessity, some grandparents are working the full-time job of caregivers.

What an opportunity!

Parenting is life under a microscope—every action seems to be scrutinized and magnified, studied and analyzed. Parents are concerned about character and learning, morals and manners. They have the daily pressures of provision and protection and sometimes they are very overwhelmed. In the moments of parenting, sometimes the big picture is lost to the present set of circumstances for both the child and the parent.

If parenting is the microscope, then grandparenting is life through a telescope. They have looked up from the microscope and seen their parenting survive. Their children have gone on to have their own children and the grandparents who are engaged in the daily aspects of the second generation can teach those children things with a fresh perspective. They see the passage of time not in moments, but in years. They have loved and lost; they have experienced hope and discouragement, and they know the sun still rises and life's rhythm continues.

For those who have the ability to speak into the lives of the second generation, take those opportunities to teach them diligently; teach them about how God is good and decisions can be tough; regrets are hard and right is rewarding. Teach them the holiness that comes from walking with God and pass a legacy of love to those who are connected to you—to those you have loved since the moment you found out your children were having children. Show them the world through the telescope—it's a big place and they need you to show them the wonder and the dangers and give them another voice to heed that loves them more than they know and cares more than they can fathom.

Thought-provoker:

Whether we are daily grandparents or holiday ones, how are we engaging in the lives of the second generation? If not a grandparent yet, into whom can we invest our experience and hope?

Abba, thank You for the opportunity to share the bigger picture of life with the second generation. Please help us be a good influence no matter what our grandparent status may be. And help us not take for granted the unique perspective You have given us to share. In Jesus' name, Amen.

Notes/Insights:

The Dump Truck Driver

> "'Bring all the tithes into the storehouse, That there may be food in My house, And try Me now in this,' Says the Lord of hosts, 'If I will not open for you the windows of heaven And pour out for you such blessing That there will not be room enough to receive it.'"
> Malachi 3:10 NKJV

Part of the renovations at our home required a dump truck filled with gravel. Despite my age and "maturity," I was excited to see the truck. As it rolled up the driveway, I went out to meet the driver. He asked where I wanted the gravel dumped. We had set a specific place with the contractor about where the gravel should be dropped, but the driver explained that the gravel would not fit in the area we had chosen. He said if he dropped it there, it would spill over—into the grass, on the driveway, and once he had started the drop, he would not be able to stop the gravel from spilling out. I told him to go ahead and dump it and we would see what happened.

He pulled into the area with the big truck and I noticed the tires left some ruts. The driver swung out of the cab, undid a few cables and chains, and then he pulled the lever. The truck bed started to rise, the back door shifted open and the gravel came. It spilled over the top of the pile and kept spreading as more and more gravel poured out. The gravel did exactly what the driver said—it overflowed the area we had chosen and spread over the grass and onto the driveway.

God's blessings are like that gravel, and He is the truck driver. He tells us to faithfully obey His Word, and He is ready and willing to pour out a truckload of blessings. Gravel may not seem like a blessing, but it was the foundation for a new room in our home. It became part of the driveway that welcomes others to our place, and it became an illustration of how God pours out generously into the hearts of those who obey Him.

And the ruts? They reminded me that once God dumps a load of blessings, we are never the same. Whenever I mow the lawn, I bounce in the seat as I go over the ruts, and it makes me smile. They remind me of the wonderful day the gravel was poured out and our home was changed. The ruts remind me to be grateful for the gravel, and for the truck driver who brought the blessings in an overflowing abundance and knew just where to dump it.

Thought-provoker:

Are we obeying the Lord and His Word? Have you seen the truckload of blessings He is so willing to pour out on our lives? Are we grateful for the gravel?

Lord, thank You for the truckload of blessings, and the ruts of gratefulness in our lives to remember that all good things come from You. In Jesus' name, Amen.

Notes/Insights:

The Electrician

"God has spoken once, twice I have heard this: that power belongs to God. Also to You, O Lord, belongs mercy; for You render to each one according to his work."

Psalm 62:11-12 NKJV

During the renovations on our house, one of the skilled workers we needed was an electrician. He came to the house, figured out where the receptacles and outlets needed to be, drew a plan and then installed the necessary equipment and wiring for electricity to flow into the house. Even with all his skill, the electric company still had to come out and open the access to the wiring from their pole to our home in order for power to flow into the house.

According to the text for today, the "power belongs to God." He is the electric company, so to speak, as He holds the power in His hands—the power of life and death, the power of breath, the power to live, and move and have our being—all comes from Him. So, how does that power flow into our lives? How do we tap into His resources and draw strength for every part of our "life house"? For believers, the electrician is the Holy Spirit. He conducts the power of God into our hearts and lives. Like our electrician, He knows how to connect the wiring and get the power from heaven to us. Through His Word, He tells us how it works. The Word tells us without Him, we can do nothing (John 15).

That makes us the electric appliances. Without power, we sit; we cannot even push our own power button. My toaster does not magically make toast without power. My coffee pot cannot run unless I plug it in and turn it on. We are the same—without God's power we aren't doing anything meaningful. Oh, we may be sitting on the counter, but we aren't getting the breakfast made. We may be pretty accessories, but without His power, we don't get the job done. Yet, with His power, even the least attractive appliance has purpose.

No one has ever said, "That's a very attractive waffle iron you have." But, no one complains when I use the waffle iron to make the tastiest cinnamon waffles on a cold morning. Each appliance gains its meaning and purpose when it plugs into the power source and turns on to its purpose. It makes no difference whether we sit on the kitchen counter, or we are pulled out once a week from the shelf, when we get plugged in, we make the meal that brings others together so they can enjoy the blessings of God.

Thought-provoker:

Are we plugged into God's power through the Holy Spirit, or are we just sitting, doing nothing?

Father, thank You that the power belongs to You and You are so willing and gracious to power us to the purpose You have deemed for each of us. Please help us to be plugged into Your Spirit today and to do things that have meaning and purpose for Your honor and glory. In Jesus' name, Amen.

Notes/Insights:

The Emergency Room Nurse

> "'When did we see You a stranger and take You in, or naked and clothe You? Or when did we see You sick, or in prison, and come to You?' And the King will answer and say to them, 'Assuredly, I say to you, inasmuch as you did it to one of the least of these My brethren, you did it to Me.'"
>
> Matthew 25:38-41 NKJV

Two of my good friends are emergency room nurses. They have been through a lot of schooling, training and experiences that have given them the ability to stay calm under pressure, to follow protocols under pressure and to be able to think during crises. They are gifted to be able to decipher between critical and necessary treatment and to provide treatment in life-threatening situations. Chaos, noise and bodily fluids do not deter them from showing up and working hard day after day. They are not turned off by messiness or pain. They understand their job is to intervene medically for the good of the patient, not just feel sorry or worry for them. They can function on little or no sleep and they are prepared to handle whatever emergency comes through the ER doors. Crisis moments are their specialties.

Crisis moments—those times when life becomes more than we can handle; the days when our hearts are bleeding from spiritual battles or poor choices. Times when we would prefer to be left alone, but our souls are hemorrhaging and we are bleeding out emotionally, or we are in dire physical need. Those who are part of God's hospital, the church, are to be like these ER nurses. When people are in dire straights, when they have nowhere else to turn, they will come to the ER.

They will show up on a Sunday morning in the foyer at church, they will send us a text or they will leave us a voicemail and they need us to be calm in the midst of their crises. God asks us to be there, to show up and to act in moments of crisis.

"When did we see You a stranger…clothe You…help You…visit You?" The questions Jesus poses for those who follow Him. We do those things when people are in crisis. ER nurses don't get to work a convenient eight-hour shift—their work begins the moment the ER door opens. Sometimes, that is in the middle of the night, on a holiday or when they are exhausted. We don't get to choose when crises occur, but we do get to choose whether we will be there, show up and act for His glory.

Ever notice that most people don't remember the names of the nurses that helped them, but they speak well of the hospital where they were treated? Same for us. Being about the Father's business isn't about fame or name recognition—it's about helping in times of crisis so others speak well of Him.

Thought-provoker:

How are we showing up and taking action when others are in crisis? Does it matter if they remember who we are?

Father, thank You for the opportunity to help others in crisis. May we remember it's about them finding You and not about us. In Jesus' name, Amen.

Notes/Insights:

The Engineer

"'For My thoughts are not your thoughts, nor are your ways My ways,' says the Lord. 'For as the heavens are higher than the earth, so are My ways higher than your ways, and My thoughts than your thoughts.'"

Isaiah 55:8-9 NKJV

I am happily married to the best man on the planet for me. God knew exactly what He was doing when He put a creative, teacher-type with an analytical engineer. We keep each other balanced; we have enjoyed many joyful experiences and endured many difficult ones together. We are blessed beyond measure to do this life together. One thing I will not ever be able to understand, though, is the language my husband speaks when he is working. Engineering has its own vocabulary and acronyms and, unless you are a part of that world, it is difficult to understand. I was talking with another engineer's wife the other day and she said, "When he decided to become an engineer, he started speaking in alphabet—CME this, or NOE that. I had to just nod and smile and know that he knew what he was doing."

My husband, however, knows the vocabulary. He can decipher the acronyms. He understands that alphabet. He can use that language to build networks and allow people to communicate with each other in ways that were only a thought within a dream just a few years ago. He has the ability to bring wires and screens to life with connections. My husband's best friend uses that language to build bridges and roads. We were allowed, one time, to drive on a road he had designed and overseen before the public even knew what it looked like. We have seen bridges he has built and he has been moved all over the country to build roads and bridges for others who have no idea where to begin.

God engineers life, and as He does, there will be things we will not understand. As He speaks the language of integrating joy with sorrow, hurt with healing, we do not always understand the vocabulary. As He builds hope, connects hearts and creates compassion, we may not be able to decipher the acronyms. Just like we do not have to know all the things an engineer knows to see that he does good work, so we will not understand all that God is doing, and yet, we know He is good. As He engineers your life and mine, we can trust Him, and we should, because He is putting together things we could never imagine. Thank Him for the bridges, the networks and the connections He is creating for you and know He does all things well.

Thought-provoker:

Are we struggling to understand the mysteries of God's engineering or are we trusting He knows what He is doing and He does all things well?

Father, thank You that You understand the vocabulary of life-engineering and You always do the best work. Help us trust when we cannot see, help us hope when we hurt, knowing You are a good, good Father and You know what You are doing. In Jesus' name, Amen.

Notes/Insights:

The Tow Truck Driver

> "She said, 'No one, Lord.' And Jesus said to her, 'Neither do I condemn you; go and sin no more.' Then Jesus spoke to them again, saying, 'I am the light of the world. He who follows Me shall not walk in darkness, but have the light of life.'"
>
> John 8:11-12 NKJV

When you are sitting on the side of the road with a broken-down car, you are grateful to see the yellow lights. The light bar of yellow means the tow truck has arrived. When the tow truck comes, the driver doesn't ask you how you have been treating your car, or if you were speeding. He gets some basic information and gets your car hooked up to the truck so he can give you a lift to a safer place and get your car somewhere for repairs.

Sometimes, when a tow truck arrives, the car is in shambles. Perhaps it was a bad accident, the car caught fire, the engine has blown or there is something beyond repair. The best thing he can do is take the car to a junk lot and leave it for scrap metal. Other times, the brokenness can be fixed and the car is worth keeping—it just needs some repair work. In each of these cases, it is not the tow truck driver's job to discern the decision about the vehicle, he is just supposed to get the driver to safety and the car off the road.

God asks us, at times, to be tow truck drivers. When someone's life is stuck on the side of the road, He asks us to give him a ride. It is not our job to grill the driver about the car—his/her past. We are to get them to safety and allow the Lord to decide if they need to completely forsake their past and start a new life, or if the life they are living just needs some repairing and improvement to get running again. Demanding answers from the driver makes them feel uneasy and unsettled. We help the most by getting them to a safe place where they can make decisions about God's offer of redemption, future choices and present circumstances without judgment or criticism. The driver already knows his life is roadside; he needs the assurance that others will help him get on the road again. Tow truck drivers do that. They give others a lift so they can get back on the road again. Whether it is a new start or repentance that leads to life repairs—that decision belongs to the Great Mechanic, Jesus, not the tow truck drivers. But, getting them to His repair shop is our job—so let's get moving on that today.

Thought-provoker:

Are we towing others to Jesus with love or condemnation? How do we get back to driving again if our lives are the ones that are roadside?

Lord, thank You for the privilege to help others get to You without judgment and condemnation. Help us to love them to You today. In Jesus' name, Amen.

Notes/Insights:

The Event Planner

> "Then the King will say to those on His right hand, 'Come, you blessed of My Father, inherit the kingdom prepared for you from the foundation of the world.'"
>
> Matthew 25:34 NKJV

I had the opportunity to be an event planner twice last year—two weddings, a sister and a dear friend. It was an honor to be trusted by each of the brides and I did my best to make sure their special days were exactly what they had hoped they would be. Since this is not my profession, I spent time with a professional event planner and learned from her wisdom and experience. She gave great advice, the most important piece being, "Prepare for everything and hope it doesn't all happen at once."

Prepare for everything—I sat down and thought about every contingency. What to do if the weather did not cooperate, who should cover in case of an illness in the bridal party, how to restructure the reception if the caterer was late—all of these possibilities were thought of and contingency plans were made. What I did not do was go over every possible catastrophe with the bride and groom. They had enough to plan on their own with colors, place settings, food, etc. I kept the contingency plans to myself, hoping they would not be necessary, and thankfully, most of them were not.

God is the pinnacle event planner. He set all the lives of billions of people into His orchestrated story we call history, and He knows the exact outcome—His kingdom prepared since the foundation of the world. He planned for every contingency—man's rebellion, Satan's attacks, wicked world rulers, humble servants—and His events will go as planned. Redemption, through the blood of Christ on the cross, was His idea. Just like an event planner, He has kept some of His plans to Himself and He will reveal them as needed. What we need to know—we can trust Him.

The weddings were special, for both the brides and for me. The work, the planning, the fulfilling of the brides' wishes on their special days were all part of special memories for each of us. The brides were thrilled because they were starting their new journeys with their husbands with love and excitement. For me, seeing the day come and all those good plans become reality was my heartfelt satisfaction. I can only imagine how the Father's heart will swell on the day He ushers us into the kingdom He has prepared, before the foundations of the world, and says, "Welcome!"

Thought-provoker:

Are you a part of the Father's plans or are you standing outside the kingdom? What steps do you need to take today to be a part of His kingdom?

Father, thank You that You are preparing an eternity with great love and care for us. Please help us to be a part of Your plan and not an outsider. Help us to bring others into Your kingdom too, so we can enjoy eternity together. In Jesus' name, Amen.

Notes/Insights:

The Firefighter

> "Jesus told him, 'I am the way, the truth, and the life. No one comes to the Father except through Me. If you know Me, you will also know My Father. From now on you do know Him and have seen Him.'"
>
> John 14:6 NLT

A friend of ours is the captain of our local fire station. Now, Gary is a nice guy—very friendly and easy to get to know. He enjoys life and he has a great sense of humor—until it comes to a fire. He takes fires seriously. He has been trained how to rescue people, how to put out fires and prevent damage. He knows how to drive a fire truck; he drives safely at high speeds and knows what to do when he gets to the scene. He can assess the situation quickly and knows what is the best way to put the fire out and save lives.

Imagine you are in a burning building. You wake up in a panic because you smell smoke. You find there are flames and smoke all around you and you are scared. You are not sure which way it is to get to safety and you definitely have no way of putting out the fire. When the firefighter comes in to rescue you, he doesn't give you an option. He picks you up and carries you out of the burning building. You don't stop to discuss how you are going to be rescued, you don't get to decide what you think is the best way to save you. The firefighter comes in and tells you this is how you are going to be rescued and he does the work of getting you out.

Jesus is the eternal firefighter. Like Gary, Jesus is friendly and loves life. He celebrated weddings with friends and spent time with children. But, He takes sin-fires seriously. He knows the way to safety because He designed it. He comes in and rescues us from the burning building of sin through His work on the cross. He tells us He is the Way; we don't get to decide how we are going to be rescued.

When we are in trouble, when we are in the midst of the fire, we need to be rescued. We need someone who knows the plan and we turn to Him to save us from the fire and get us to safety. We must trust He said what He meant and He loves us so much, He was willing to die for us. We need to stop trying to save ourselves and rely on Him—The Way—to rescue us. And we are grateful, because we wouldn't be able to save ourselves from the fire.

Thought-provoker:

Are we arguing with the eternal Firefighter about our rescue or do we trust Him and His redemption design? What do we need to surrender today so He can rescue us?

Father, thank You for Your plan of salvation. Help us remember it's Your plan and we need to trust You to save us. In Jesus' name, Amen.

Notes/Insights:

The Florist

> "But God, who is rich in mercy, because of His great love with which He loved us, even when we were dead in trespasses, made us alive together with Christ (by grace you have been saved), and raised us up together, and made us sit together in the heavenly places in Christ Jesus."
>
> Ephesians 2:4-6 NKJV

I really enjoy flowers. I have no talent, whatsoever, for arranging them, but I so enjoy seeing how others put them together to make a beautiful bouquet. I admire how they combine colors, textures and plants to make stunning arrangements and they make them appropriate to the occasion. Florists take different flowers, weeds to some, and combine them into something lovely. A flower in the field may go unnoticed, but it becomes a centerpiece in the hands of the good florist. Certain types of floral arrangements are sent to funerals, while others are sent to weddings, retirements, or celebrations. Flowers can be sent for Christmas, Mother's Day, Veterans Day and other holidays, and each arrangement suits the occasion.

Florists are amazing people. They use their creativity and artistic expression to make beautiful things out of things that are dying. Yes, cut flowers and stems are dying, yet florists arrange them in such a way that their beauty and vibrancy shows instead of their inevitable withering away.

Through the power of grace and mercy, God is the ultimate florist. He takes us —simple specimens like grass or weeds (James 4)—and makes us into beautiful arrangements as testimony to His goodness. He arranges each of us individually, and as a larger body as the church—into bouquets of beauty for the world to admire. He not only takes us and makes us vibrant; He also makes us alive again. Florists do their best to make flowers pretty and last for a few days or a week—God revives us and makes us alive again in Him (Colossians 2:13). He takes us from the unnoticed fields of humanity; He places us in His kingdom, for His glory, and gives each of us a purpose. Whether we are the centerpiece flower given a place of influence, or we are the supporting stems through our prayers and giving, each part fills in the space in His bouquet to make a beautiful piece of art. Each flower and stem is needed to make the bouquet what the florist wants it to be and God needs each of His flowers, us, to take our places in His arrangements so His will can be accomplished. In the hands of the Florist, we are alive and beautiful.

Thought-provoker:

Are we allowing God to arrange us as He sees fit to make us a beautiful part of His bouquet? What do we need to do today to be a part of His arrangement?

Father, thank You for arranging us to make us beautiful pieces of testimony for Your glory. Help us to enjoy the place You put us so Your bouquet comes out exactly as You want it. In Jesus' name, Amen.

Notes/Insights:

The Funeral Director

"Even when we are weighed down with troubles, it is for your comfort and salvation! For when we ourselves are comforted, we will certainly comfort you. Then you can patiently endure the same things we suffer."

2 Corinthians 1:6 NLT

He was soft-spoken and calm. As he went about the responsibilities of helping our friends, he gave advice and was helpful without being intrusive. He brought tissues when they were needed, and he wrote things down to help the family remember their decisions. He walked them through the decisions of words, order and actions for a memorial service that would honor their loved one. He gave them suggestions as they lacked the presence of mind as emotions took over. His presence helped them through one of the most difficult times in life—he had compassion on the living as he prepared their loved one's body for the cemetery.

I wondered how someone would choose such a profession. As I watched him work, my curiosity rose. How did he know what to do, what to say, how to help? I had the opportunity to talk with him while our friends were taking a moment to gather their emotions as a family. So, I asked. His response: "My father taught me this business." His father had decided to learn the ins and outs of the funeral business after a hard family loss. This young man had watched his father comfort and help others through all kinds of loss. Through the years, they had witnessed all kinds of suffering—and yet, he chose to comfort. He chose to honor those who had been taken. He chose to help families in times of crisis and to advise those who faced the future alone. By enduring the deep loss in his own life, his father was able to use his experiences to know what, and what not, to do, say and be during times of loss. And he had passed this wisdom onto his son.

Our heavenly Father is teaching us this business too. Not the funeral business, but the business of comfort. As we experience hurts and losses in this life, we are better equipped to help others navigate when their times of loss come. But, just like the funeral director, we must learn how to comfort—we must be sure we are helping, not hurting, the process. How do we do that? By watching how our Father comforts us during difficult times, and be willing to act like Him when we help others. The experiences God has placed in our lives give us the ability to reach out and hold those who are going through the same pain; to comfort, to honor and to know—these are blessings that come through loss. Blessings the Funeral Director knew how to share, and ones we can share as well.

Thought-provoker:

What losses have made us better comforters? Do we thank God for those experiences? Are we sharing comfort with others?

Lord, thank You that our losses are never wasted as You use them in us to help us comfort others. Help us to do so today. In Jesus' name, Amen.

Notes/Insights:

The Travel Agent

> "Now then, we are ambassadors for Christ, as though God were pleading through us: we implore you on Christ's behalf, be reconciled to God."
>
> 2 Corinthians 5:20 NKJV

It's all about connecting flights, hotels, and showing people the best way to get where they want to go. Tara has the privilege of being a travel agent. People come to her for various reasons—they need to book a business trip, they want to go on vacation, they want to surprise someone else with the trip of a lifetime—but all of them come to her seeking direction.

Tara's job is to point them in the right direction. She is also there if the travel plans change due to bad weather or road construction. Her clients can contact her at any time, and she will help them find the way to get to their destination. She finds the travel solutions, makes the reservations and even gives them payment options, but it is up to her clients to take the trip. Tara cannot force them to get in the rental car or get on the plane—she can only point them in the direction they should go.

We are spiritual travel agents. We are to be pointing people to their spiritual destination—a glorious eternity with the Creator of the universe. We are to be showing others His love and pointing them toward the Redeemer of the world. People will come into our lives for various reasons—family members, friends, even business partners—and we are to give them the information about the trip of a lifetime; the journey to a final destination in Heaven itself. All of those around us are seeking direction, and it's our job to point them to the right way.

There will be times when others will look to us in times of difficulty. When the storms of life alter their journey, or when the trials of life obstruct them from reaching goals or having hope, they will look to us. Just like Tara, we need to be available to show them the solutions found in God's Word and help them reroute toward a relationship with Him, not from Him.

And we need to be gracious. We can show them the Way (John 14:6), we can show them the reservations (Romans 10:9-10) and we can even show them the payment plan (Romans 5:8), but it is up to them if they want to join the journey (John 3:16). As they make their decisions, we need to be like Tara. She waits for the phone call from her clients to book the trip. She knows when they make the decision, they will commit to the journey and have the trip of a lifetime. We want the same for those around us when it comes to their spiritual destinations too.

Thought-provoker:

Are we sharing the travel solutions of a Savior with those who are traveling through life with us? Make today a good travel agent day—share the destination with someone and pray they commit to the journey.

Father, thank You that we represent the One who holds the eternal destination of Heaven for all who choose to come. Help us share with those around us today. In Jesus' name, Amen.

Notes/Insights:

The Graffiti Artist

> "Do you not know that the unrighteous will not inherit the kingdom of God? Do not be deceived. Neither fornicators, nor idolaters, nor adulterers, nor homosexuals, nor sodomites, nor thieves, nor covetous, nor drunkards, nor revilers, nor extortioners will inherit the kingdom of God. And such were some of you. But you were washed, but you were sanctified, but you were justified in the name of the Lord Jesus and by the Spirit of our God."
>
> I Corinthians 6:9-11 NKJV

It is an honest, legal job. It may seem unusual, but a legal graffiti artist is commissioned by certain cities to paint walls, bridges or other big objects throughout the cities. The hope is that the true art from the legal artist will deter others from marring the city landscape with unsightly or vulgar types of graffiti.

The problem for the true graffiti artist is that others will come along after his work is complete and mar the picture. They will add their own version to the artist's story, or they will ruin his picture completely. They do not respect the time, talent and effort the artist put into the work; they think their additions are more important, but they destroy the true art already in place. And so, the true artist must work again, and attempt to restore the beauty of his own work.

God has a beautiful plan. He thought out His plan very well and He crafted a beautiful picture—He calls it marriage. God wove the colors of love, faithfulness, fidelity, hope and laughter within marriage. He took the time to write down what He thinks of marriage and how it should look. Within marriage, God wove the picture of His Beloved Son and the Son's bride, the church. He wants His picture to be perfect, but there are some who do not like His artwork. They think they know how to improve the picture with their own version of what it should be. They take their spray can of ideas and they mar the true picture of marriage. They do not respect God and His wisdom, they think they know better than He and they wind up destroying the true art of God's illustration.

God approved of His art long ago. As the Creator, He deemed marriage a good thing. When Satan mars it, or the selfishness of someone ruins the true picture, it is heartbreaking. When the flagrant marks of rebellion within a culture, or the slashes of pride are sprayed across marriage, it mars it. But because God is a wonderful artist, He works to restore that picture time and again. It would be worth it if, instead of marring the picture, we admired His true art and kept His ideas of marriage and love with the utmost respect for the Artist who designed it.

Thought-provoker:
What ideas are we allowing that mar the beautiful art of marriage in our own lives and in our culture? What should we do to show the world the respect and reverence for marriage it so desperately needs to see?

Lord, thank You that marriage is Your idea and it is a great one. Help us to uphold the picture of Your Son and His bride and show others how beautiful You designed marriage to be. In Jesus' name, Amen.

Notes/Insights:

The Hair Stylist

"Let no corrupting talk come out of your mouths, but only such as is good for building up, as fits the occasion, that it may give grace to those who hear."

Ephesians 4:29 ESV

She is one of my best acquaintances. Even though I only see her once every six to eight weeks, I look forward to our visits. She is very well trained in her trade, and her skills help me to feel more confident and prepared as I go about doing my calling. She usually spends about an hour with me, and her perky personality and perceptive insights help to bring out the best in me. Well, at least the best in my hair--she is my hair stylist.

She does a great job of matching my hairstyle to my personality. When I decided I wanted to go short, she gave me a sleek bob. When I decided to let my hair grow long, she kept the bangs trimmed and the ends tipped so they would grow. When I was in between the short and the long styles, and frustrated by the lack of progress, she encouraged me to wait it out a little longer and not make a rash decision. I am glad she was persuasive, because eight weeks later, my hair was touching my shoulders and back in my good graces. She listens to me and asks questions about what is going on in my life. She intuitively senses if I need a change, a boost in confidence that she can provide with a new look, or if I just need a little tune-up. She can even tell if I need some "pampering"—a wash and condition along with a blow dry and style, or if I am doing well and just need a cut-and-go.

When I leave her place, I feel pretty and confident and willing to take on the world. She gives me the instructions and shows me the methods I need to be able to replicate her styling when I get home. And every eight weeks, she does it again to help me feel good about my appearance.

We should be the hair stylists of the Christian realm. No, I am not asking any of you to pick up your scissors and attempt to change my look. I am referring to the instilling of confidence and paying attention to the needs of others around us. We should hear the weariness in others' voices, be perceptive of discouragement or frustration, and we should encourage them back to their confidence in Christ. Sometimes, we need to "pamper" a discouraged friend—go the extra mile, do something special for him, or let her know she is loved and is needed as a member of the family of God. Be a hair stylist—go restore someone's confidence.

Thought-provoker:
Are we encouraging others and restoring confidence in God in those around us?

Lord, help us to see those who are discouraged and be willing to come alongside. In Jesus' Name, Amen.

Notes/Insights:

The Usher

"One thing have I asked of the Lord, that will I seek after: that I may dwell in the house of the Lord all the days of my life, to gaze upon the beauty of the Lord and to inquire in his temple."

Psalm 27:4 ESV

There is an older gentleman who is an usher at one of the venues I attend on occasion. With dark skin and snow-white hair, dark brown eyes and a smile that lights up a room, he is a part of the experience I look forward to when we go to the auditorium. Even his uniform is sharp and crisp and makes it easy to find him. If you have a question about seating, the venue, or the program, he is the man to see. He is observant and helpful—he asks questions to help guide you without being intrusive and he attends to needs he can meet from his post. He makes a good first impression for the event staff, and what is more impressive to me is that he continues that first impression experience even after he knows your name and has seen you at several events.

Another thing I like about this gentleman is that he does not leave his post during the event. While others are enjoying the speaker, the concert or some other event—he is right there enjoying it along with us. He is attentive to his section of the auditorium and makes sure we are enjoying our experience, but his smile lets you know he is enjoying the event as well. And, as we leave, he always shares a "Come back and see us soon" with a wave and genuine expression. We know he really would like us to come back again.

An usher—a seemingly simple job on one hand, and such an important one on so many levels on the other. He is the face of the organization that plans the events. His tone, body language, even appearance, all set the impressions of the event in motion. What if each of us understood our position as an usher in the kingdom of God?

We are the point of contact for those in our section of life. We are the first impression they have of our heavenly Father and His design for the events of a lifetime. We are the ones who should be answering their questions, being helpful without being intrusive and attending to the needs we can meet. We should be enjoying the will of God right along with them as we stay in His will, and we should be encouraging others to come back again and again to enjoy fellowship with us and the Father in His house. We believers are all part of the event staff of God—let's do our best to be consistent at pointing others to their seats and meeting their needs in the kingdom today.

Thought-provoker:

How are we doing as ushers in the kingdom? Who is in our sections today that need our help?

Father, thank You that we have the privilege of representing You. Help us do a good job at our posts each day so others can come into Your kingdom and Your family. In Jesus' name, Amen.

Notes/Insights:

The Kindergarten Teacher

> "I therefore, a prisoner for the Lord, urge you to walk in a manner worthy of the calling to which you have been called, with all humility and gentleness, with patience, bearing with one another in love, eager to maintain the unity of the Spirit in the bond of peace."
>
> Ephesians 4:1-3 ESV

Twenty-five years. For twenty-five years, she poured a love of learning, a gentle spirit and patience into her Kindergarten classroom. I am privileged to know her as "Grammie Van." She spent twenty-five years loving on young ones as they learned their phonics, basic math skills and love of science. She walked them through early American history and made the forefathers come alive off the page as she taught her students interesting facts and silly legends. She taught her kindergartners to think, to wonder, to work hard and to love the process of discovery. She did all of this with rambunctious five and six-year-olds who could barely sit still in their seats long enough to finish a subject, let alone keep them interested for a whole day. She would let them discover bugs under rocks outside; she would teach them about leaves in the fall and flowers in the spring. She influenced hundreds of lives. She spent so many years investing in the lives of others.

I have a picture of Grammie that I just absolutely adore. When our daughter was little—just learning to read, Grammie grabbed a book and asked Charity to join her in the rocking chair in the living room. There, in those few precious moments, Grammie passed on her legacy—her love of learning intertwined with patience and gentleness as she read into another young life and instilled another moment of love in one of her students.

I am thankful for the Grammies in each of our lives. Those who were gifted to teach us with love, humility and grace as they invested in our lives and opened new doors of learning for us. Each kindergarten teacher who loves what they do and loves the students they teach—invests in eternity. For as their students learn to read and think, they give their students the opportunity to read God's Word and learn more of the Savior who loves them.

Did Grammie ever win a national teacher's award? No, and she wouldn't have wanted it anyway. She would want to be remembered simply as the Kindergarten teacher who loves each and every one of her students and hopes that each has passed on a love of learning as they walk through life. May we all have the spirit of a Kindergarten teacher as we share with others.

Thought-provoker:

Are we sharing love, humility and grace to those around us like a Kindergarten teacher? Is there someone we need to thank for the love of learning they invested in each of us? Tell them today.

Lord, thank You for the Kindergarten teachers who have invested in our lives and given us a love to learn. Help us to have their spirit today. In Jesus' name, Amen.

Notes/Insights:

The Landscaper

> "To all who mourn in Israel, he will give a crown of beauty for ashes, a joyous blessing instead of mourning, festive praise instead of despair. In their righteousness, they will be like great oaks that the Lord has planted for his own glory."
>
> Isaiah 61:3 NLT

Louis can look at an empty dirt plot and see a beautiful park. He looks at a blank space in the landscape and his mind's eye sees lush grass, trees, a park bench and a walking trail. He can also look at a weed-driven, overgrown lawn and picture a cultivated yard with a manicured flowerbed under the front windows.

As a landscaper, it's Louis' job to see what isn't there. When a contractor calls him to the site of a new construction, there is usually a lot of dirt. Piles of it. The grass is nowhere to be found. Yet, as Louis walks the lot with the contractor, he starts to formulate a plan for hedges under the windows, flowers by the front door and grass. Louis knows what types of plants will grow well in the sun, in the shade and in between. He knows the names of plants I have never heard of and he has a natural knack for putting colors together that highlight the land and beautify the space.

When the contractor allows Louis freedom to work, the results are amazing. What was once a mournful lot of lowliness transforms into a yard fit for the nicest family or the wealthiest executive. But, when a client interferes with Louis's plan, the results are short-circuited. When the client demands pink flowers where red and yellow would serve better, it diminishes the view. Louis doesn't force his ideas on anyone, and he will allow the client to do whatever they wish, but he knows the end result will be less than he had dreamed and planned.

When we allow God to architect our landscape, He promises to make beauty where ashes were. That's a very impressive transformation. Ashes mean there has been fire—a purging of the land by intense heat and trial. Fire is a strong force, and it has its purpose. But, once it has done its work, it is time for the Great Landscaper to go to work. He plants hope, restoration, peace and praise in the lives of those who will leave the choice to Him, and the results are breathtaking. We must give Him the freedom to decide what the landscape will look like, but because we know how great His love is for us, we can trust His heart as He plants new, makes new paths and makes the view of our testimony beyond anything we could ask or think. Louis sees the potential beauty in a plot of dirt. God sees the potential glory in a broken heart. Trust Him with yours today.

Thought-provoker:

Are we allowing God to fill the landscape of our lives with His glory and praise? Are we trusting Him with our broken hearts?

Father, thank You that You make beauty from ashes. When we trust You with the results, our broken hearts will works of beautiful amazement that will bring You glory. Help us to believe that today and tomorrow too. In Jesus' name, Amen.

Notes/Insights:

The Locksmith

"I am He who lives, and was dead, and behold, I am alive forevermore. Amen. And I have the keys of Hades and of Death. Write the things which you have seen, and the things which are, and the things which will take place after this."

Revelation 1:18-19 NKJV

A miscommunication about who was still at home meant that the exterior doors of the house were locked while I was out in the back, and when I came back to the house, I could not get inside. Fortunately, I was able to contact one of our children and he was able to bring back a key to let me back in the house. When I was telling the story at church, I found out one of our friends is a locksmith. A conversation about what he does and how he does it revealed very interesting information.

The first thing Ronnie has realized about his job is that most of his clients call when they are upset or panicked. Ronnie has learned to be a calming force, to not allow the circumstances to rattle him, and to come to the aid of his clients. He cares about them and their situations, and he is willing to provide the solutions. Second, Ronnie knows he has the solution. He has the skill set, and the tools, to be able to help his clients. Whether it is a lawyer locked out of the building or a mom panicked because the baby is locked in the car, Ronnie works the same. And, lastly, Ronnie is good at what he does. It does not take him long to assess the situation, determine what is needed, and "pop the lock."

Jesus is the great locksmith. He knows we are locked out of heaven without redemption, and He is the only One who can "pop that lock." When He came, He knew what His mission was and He knew He was the solution to our sin problem. He did not get distracted and He had no need for panic. He cared for us, even when we were unlovable (Romans 5:7-9). Jesus is the best at what He does. In fact, He is the only One who can do it (Acts 4:12).

Jesus hears the calls and fears of those who realize they are locked out of heaven, and He comes. He cares and He unlocks the door for us (John 3:16). He is willing for all to come in and, according to today's text, He still holds the keys so no one can lock the door and keep us out. Do you need an eternal door opened? Call the eternal locksmith—Jesus will come, and He knows just what you need.

Thought-provoker:
Are we attempting to force eternal doors open, or are we willing to allow Jesus to open them for us?

Father, thank You for opening the doors of heaven through Your Son, Jesus Christ. Help us to show others Your love and that You hold the keys. In Jesus' name, Amen.

Notes/Insights:

The Make Up Artist

> "Put on then, as God's chosen ones, holy and beloved, compassionate hearts, kindness, humility, meekness, and patience, bearing with one another and, if one has a complaint against another, forgiving each other; as the Lord has forgiven you, so you also must forgive. And above all these put on love, which binds everything together in perfect harmony."
>
> Colossians 3:12-14 ESV

My sister is a beauty consultant. In addition to doing make up, she also knows about skin conditioning, protection and nutrition. She knows about acne products, dry skin emollients and sunscreen and how each product works with another to improve skin on a cellular level as well as its appearance.

Maybe you can relate—sometimes, I am very angry with my skin. Stress, a cheat on my wellness plan, an allergy or even a slight hormone imbalance all show on my skin. When I am getting ready for a big event, my skin will get oily. If there is a change in weather, rosacea flares. When I am trying to take on the world, a breakout occurs. In these moments, I rely on my sister's wisdom and expertise to help. With all her knowledge, she cannot make the flares or the breakouts go away, but she patiently talks me through the process of treating and covering them. If she is in the area, she will drop in and work her make up magic herself. If she isn't, she will talk me through it over the phone. When I complain about my skin, she has a solution. And her results are always fabulous. Because she knows the products, and she knows me, she makes good results happen.

God is like that too. God knows all about the traits that will make us beautiful. He knows our flaws; He knows what causes our temperaments to flare and what causes us to be angry. He knows how badly we feel about ourselves and how angry we can be with who we are when we are stressed or hurting. He also knows applying kindness, compassion, humility and meekness to our lives makes us lovely again.

His make-up is for the heart, and it affects our appearances too. As we allow Him to apply compassion for others, our faces will soften. When He applies kindness, our smiles return. When He adds humility and meekness, our cheeks change from an angry red to a peachy hue. As He gently rubs forgiveness into our lives, the scars fade. When we put on His love, our faces become radiant. Without the heart make up of God, we are quite the sight. But, when He adds His love and grace, we become beautiful testimonies of what happens when we trust the true artist to bring out our beauty. Because God knows how His "products" work, and because He knows us, He makes good results happen. Allow Him to do the applying today.

Thought-provoker:

What heart make up do we need God to apply today to make us lovely again?

Lord, thank You that You know exactly what we need to be lovely and You give it to us willingly. Help us apply it so Your love and grace shine through. In Jesus' name, Amen.

Notes/Insights:

The Mechanic

"He heals the brokenhearted and binds up their wounds."
Psalm 147:3 ESV

There are two types of mechanics in the world—ours and all the others. Tom is a true mechanic. He not only knows how to fix cars, he knows how to listen to them. I know that sounds strange, but when there is something wrong with our car, he asks me to describe the noise it is making. For Tom, there is a difference between a whizzing sound and a growl, or a hissing sound versus a vibrating hum. By listening, Tom can determine where the broken hose, worn out part or the leak is in the system. Sometimes, it is a simple repair—a hose in a system has broken because of pressure and needs to be replaced and tightened. Other times, it's a little more involved, like when a water pump decides to stop working and creates problems in others parts of the engine. Then there are those other times, when it is a major overhaul because something major has gone wrong and the whole system shuts down. You know, those tow truck moments of life. When the car has to be picked up and brought to the mechanic because it cannot get there on its own.

Tom realizes his work is more than just repairing a vehicle; he also repairs the trust the driver has in that vehicle. He communicates the problem and he gives hope that the car will run again. And when it does, he rejoices with the owner that the car is going again.

God is the heart mechanic of life. From the simple disappointments to the major crises—those tow truck moments—when a heart is so broken the owner can hardly breathe, God is there. So, what does it take to heal a broken heart? It takes listening to determine the cause. God does that—He hears our every prayer and groans with us as we hurt (Romans 8). He knows the parts of life that need fixing—He sees the injustices, the pains and the suffering, and He gently takes us into His hands and fixes those things for us. And He knows when we need a complete overhaul. He tells us there are times to rest and allow Him to totally renew us (2 Corinthians 4).

Just like Tom, God knows exactly what we need to learn to trust again. He teaches us through His healing that we can make it in this life and we learn He is the One who heals us, not some worldly mechanic, but the good heart mechanic, and He rejoices with us when the healing occurs. When your heart needs a repair, take it to the One who will fix it right.

Thought-provoker:

Who are you allowing to heal your broken heart? Whether it is a big repair or a small disappointment, take it to the One who loves you most.

Father, thank You that we can trust You to heal our broken hearts and repair our lives. Thank You that You listen, and You act to bind up our wounds and make us whole again. In Jesus' name, we thank You again. Amen.

Notes/Insights:

The Body Builder

> "Bear one another's burdens, and so fulfill the law of Christ. For if anyone thinks he is something when is nothing, he deceives himself. But let each one test his own work, and then his reason to boast will be in himself alone and not in his neighbor. For each will have to bear his own load."
>
> Galatians 6:2-5 ESV

How does one become a great body builder? Most of them start out with some level of fitness and muscle, but then they discipline themselves, and work with others, to become stronger and more capable. Today's passage starts out saying we are to bear one another's burdens, but then the end says we will each have to bear our own load. Sounds like a contradiction, but it's not. Read what is in the middle—don't be deceived. Let's break down the parallel with a weight lifter and discover the truth about body building in a spiritual sense.

We each start out "wimpy." Each of us starts as a newborn babe and we grow from there (1 Peter 2). Each of us needs others to come alongside and help us as we start our journey. Bodybuilders have coaches and spotters—people who advise them and others who stand close and are ready to help if the load becomes too heavy. But, as a body builder trains and exercises, he is able to carry more and more of the load himself.

Now, it is interesting that tucked in the middle of this passage is a warning about pride—if anyone thinks he is something, when he is nothing. This doesn't mean we have no self-worth as believers; it means if we depend on ourselves instead of our Savior, we are going to drop the load. We are going to get injured and sidelined while we wait to heal. There are tests of our work as we go along. God tests us to make us stronger, but He also tests us to make sure we are not taking on a load of self-dependence. He wants us to be able to bear our own load, but we must always remember our sufficiency is of God (2 Corinthians 3:5).

The goal of each body builder is to one day compete. In this competition, each is given the opportunity to bear up under a heavy load and be awarded for it. When he steps onto that platform, he must carry that load alone, but his coaches and spotters are watching and cheering for him. One day, God will reward His children for their loads (2 Corinthians 3). May we each accept the exercises and disciplines God has entrusted to us to make us better weight lifters and to do so to bring glory to His name.

Thought-provoker:

What spiritual workouts are building our load bearing muscles? Who are the coaches and spotters we can depend upon to help us? Where is your focus?

Father, thank you for the process of strengthening us and for those you send to coach and spot us. Help us bear our loads and depend on you. In Jesus' name, Amen.

Notes/Insights:

The Meter Reader

"Do not quench the Spirit."

1 Thessalonians 5:19 HCSB

Ava, our dog, usually sees him first. She barks furiously at the front door as he comes by once a month on a Segway. He is not an intruder; we know he has a job to do and we know why he is here. The meter reader stops at the side of our house, checks the numbers on several dials, records his findings and heads off to another house in the neighborhood.

I do not know about you, but I am thankful for the Meter Reader. He understands what the numbers and dials on the meter mean, and he gets an accurate reading so we are charged for the power we use and not the bill for the whole neighborhood. He makes sure we are only responsible for what goes on in our home when it comes to power usage.

The Holy Spirit is our spiritual meter reader. He gauges the heat of our spiritual life—are we walking firmly in the will of God, or are we sitting on the proverbial fence with the world? Sometimes, our natural nature is a lot like Ava. We sense the Holy Spirit, and we balk at His presence. We know who He is and we know why He is there. He is not an intruder—He is the God of all comfort, and He is there to help us keep our own things in order. He does not expect us to take on the responsibilities of all the other homes in our neighborhoods—that is His job.

So, what do we do with the information from the Meter Reader? Interestingly, our bill not only shows us how much we owe, but it also shows us how much power we are using.

In the physical realm, we check our power usage to be sure we are being good stewards of the money we have set aside for utilities.

Spiritually, we should not be holding back because God has given us everything we need to live out the Christian life as hot believers (I Peter 1:3-5). Notice I did not say "hot mess" believers, but "hot." We are powered by Him, engulfed in His mercy and empowered by His grace. The Holy Spirit convicts us where we need it, and He alone knows how to read the meters of spiritual growth in our lives. We need to quiet the barking of our natural natures and we need to let Him do His job and let Him show us where we need His power today.

Thought-provoker:
Are you listening to the leading of the Holy Spirit and letting Him show you where you need spiritual power today?

Lord, thank You for the spiritual readings You give us as we strive to live for You. Help us to feel Your conviction, submit to Your Spirit and accept the power You give us to live holy lives for You. In Jesus' name, Amen.

Notes/Insights:

The Middle School Teacher

> "Show yourself in all respects to be a model of good works, and in your teaching show integrity, dignity, and sound speech that cannot be condemned, so that an opponent may be put to shame, having nothing evil to say about us."
>
> Titus 2:7-8 ESV

Michelle is a middle school teacher; a history teacher in a middle school, to be exact. She is also a cheerleading sponsor and an active member of the teacher's committee. Some students would think a history teacher is a boring, introverted individual who loves to read and keep their distance, but Michelle couldn't be more the opposite.

She has the uncanny ability of connecting with students who are dealing not only with learning, but also braces, gangly limbs, pimples and hormones. She shares in their humor without harming feelings. She works with them on projects, as she oversees the learning process. She sets a good example for her students. She is always prepared for class; she plans additional adventures for them to explore and learn; she opens her door to those who need help with their assignments, and she works very hard to make sure she is an example of dignity and respect at her school. Whenever someone mentions Michelle's formal name around her students, past or present, their eyes light up and they exclaim, "Hey, I had Mrs. H-- as a history teacher. She was awesome!"

Michelle is an example of what we are to be in the world around us. The passage today says that our teaching is to show integrity. Michelle does that by being thorough and taking the time to study and prepare for her lessons. She doesn't just throw a class together and "wing it." Instead, she knows the material she is teaching and she works hard to make it interesting for her students to learn. We are to be the same kinds of teachers when it comes to God's Word and the world.

The next words in the passage are dignity and sound speech. Michelle has a very quick wit that suits her well in the environment of middle school. She sees things from a different perspective and she is capable of diffusing tensions with humor. She has always been careful to make humor from situations, not from personal characteristics. And her students love her for it. They feel safe around her because they know her speech will not be laced with insults or hurtful words. Her students respond by respecting her and by not having anything ill to say about her. Past students remember her with respect and present students, while they may not enjoy all the challenges of middle school, know there is a teacher who is supporting them through it. With these character traits—integrity, dignity and wholesome speech— we can reach and change our world. Michelle does it in the middle school world; we can do it in ours.

Thought-provoker:

What do we need to work on to make sure our testimony and teaching is a model of good works laced with integrity, dignity and sound speech? What changes do we need to make right now to make a difference in our world?

Father, help us to be the middle school teachers we should be in whatever place You have called us. We need your help and we ask You to help us start right now. In Jesus' name, Amen.

Notes/Insights:

The Mover

> "Above all, you must realize that no prophecy in Scripture ever came from the prophet's own understanding, or from human initiative. No, those prophets were moved by the Holy Spirit, and they spoke from God."
>
> 2 Peter 1:20-21 NLT

Moving day can be exciting or scary. Some moves are wanted—a husband and wife find a home because they are starting a family and need more room; a college student has landed a fantastic job after graduation and is leaving the college dorm, or a couple is down-sizing after raising their family and they are looking forward to some free time and travel without the hassle of the big house. Other moves, however, are difficult. Leaving family and friends because of a job transfer; having to move closer to a specialized hospital because of a life-threatening illness or losing a home because of a job loss or a divorce. In each of these cases, movers make the transition easier.

Movers first help us to pack. Packers come in and help to put all the things we plan to move into boxes, label them and stack them to be loaded onto the truck. The movers then load everything onto the truck and then the truck moves the stuff to the new location where the movers then take it into the new house and help with the set-up.

The Spirit does the same within our heart houses. When it is time to move, He prompts us to pack up the memories, principles and other essentials we will need for the transition. Sometimes, He asks us to change location—He asks us to trust Him and go where He is sending. Other times, He changes our ministry, our direction or our purpose. When we depend on Him during these transitions, He makes it easier because He knows where to take us and our "stuff."

Early in our marriage, a very dear mentor gave me this advice, "As you are packing up your stuff, make sure you pack up your heart too." She explained that moving with a bad attitude would make the transition much harder. Sometimes, I wonder if the prophets and apostles ever struggled with their attitudes when the Spirit moved them.

Did Jeremiah ever sigh? We know Elijah had a "kill me now" conversation with God. Did Paul ever get weary? I believe in their humanness, the answer is yes, but, they trusted their Mover to get them to where they needed to be, to settle them wherever they went and to write what they were supposed to write, so we can hold the Bible in our hands today. When the Spirit tells you it's time to move, trust His ability to get you where you need to go—He's the best mover in town.

Thought-provoker:

What is our attitude when God prompts us to move? Where is He taking us today?

Abba, thank You that You never ask us to move without You. Help us to depend on You during every transition so we get to where You want us to be. In Jesus' name, Amen.

Notes/Insights:

The Musician

"Praise ye the Lord. Sing unto the Lord a new song, and his praise in the congregation of saints."

Psalm 149:1 KJV

I am a hobby-musician. I play a few instruments and I sing in the Choir at our church, but I have not committed my life to music. But David does. He spends hours each day involved in music. He plays several instruments, he sings, he leads worship, he teaches others, he plays or sings in front of audiences each week and he works hard at his profession. He spends many hours alone, working and preparing the music he plans to sing or play. If you stop by his office, you will most likely find him working on something related to music—practicing it, listening to it, or working on a new piece of it.

Besides the time he spends alone learning and preparing, David also reads the music. This may seem terribly obvious, but there are many people who cannot read music. David has spent the time to learn what the symbols mean, how to interpret a rhythm or chord structure and how to translate that into a melody and harmony that others can enjoy. Without the skill of music reading, musicians would not understand how the song is supposed to sound and their own interpretations of it, while they may seem very good, are not what the songwriter intended. The musician needs to follow the music.

In life, we are like the musicians. Some of us may be hobby-types. We know God has a lyric written for our lives, but we are not fully committed to it and we don't spend much of our time devoted to learning the music. Others of us may be like the free spirit musicians; those who have talent and work at it, but they haven't taken the time to learn to read the music and play or sing it the way the songwriter intended. Then, there are those few who truly commit themselves to the melody God has written for their lives. They spend time in quiet, alone with God the Master Songwriter, and they prepare the notes as He has written them. They take the time to pray, prepare and read the music as it is written so their lives will be a beautiful symphony of God's timing and harmony for others to see and to enjoy. They don't interpret the music as they want; they play what God has written and His song is always lovely.

Thought-provoker:

Which type of life-musician are you? What would happen if more of us were fully committed life-musicians who played the music the way God has written it? What do we need to change to move in that direction today?

Lord, thank You for the song You have written for each of us. Help us to live the music the way it is written and help us be fully committed to the preparation of prayer and quiet time with You so we will read the music and play it well, just as it is. In Jesus' name, Amen.

Notes/Insights:

The Nutritionist

> "'All things are lawful,'" but not all things are helpful. 'All things are lawful,' but not all things build up."
> 1 Corinthians 10:23 ESV

My husband's youngest sister is a Nutritionist. She has studied the nutritional value of many different kinds of foods, as well as many human conditions, and she has learned how to recommend foods that will help the individual live healthy. Her primary goal is not weight-loss, instead she focuses on helping the individual to eat the foods that make the body work well and to stay away from foods that trigger bad immune responses or cause the body to be inflamed. Of course, this is a simplified version of what she does, but I do not have all the educational expertise to know all the ins and outs of what she does.

What I do know is she can give all the advice and expertise at her disposal, and if a diabetic patient refuses to give up sugar, his/her health will be compromised. If an obese client refuses to count calories and work aggressively at his/her weight loss goals and lifestyle change, then he/she will continue to struggle with the effects of the extra weight. She also realizes, though, that every one of her clients has the option to eat whatever they want.

There are no laws to prevent people from eating what they should not, and even with government warnings and regulations in schools, if someone wants to eat unhealthily, they will find a way. Her clients have to make the choices—the tough choices—to realize that certain foods will trigger unpleasant processes in their bodies, and some foods will make them very sick. On the other hand, if they choose to eat the healthy foods, stay away from the trigger foods and the "junk" foods that cause unhealthy reactions in their bodies, they can live healthy, active lives and enjoy the days they are given.

The Word tells us all things are lawful, meaning that no one can force us to do, or not do, certain things. The verse, however, follows up with the immediate warning, but not all things are helpful. We must realize that this freedom comes with a price. We are free to choose, but we are not free of the consequences that come with those choices. Isn't it better to give up the pound of temptation so we can achieve holiness in our lives? Isn't it better to forsake the world's junk food and fill our spiritual hearts with the life-giving lifestyle shared in the Word of God? We have that choice. And as a nutritionist, my sister-in-love would tell you—the tough choices are well worth it.

Thought-provoker:

Are we choosing things that we know are detrimental to a spiritual healthy life, or are we making the choices that are helpful? What things need to change today?

Father, thank You for the freedom of choice. Help us to choose wisely today, and every day, to live spiritually healthy lives for Your glory. In Jesus' name, Amen.

Notes/Insights:

The Optician

> "Do not love the world or the things in the world. If anyone loves the world, the love of the Father is not in him. For all that is in the world—the desires of the flesh and the desires of the eyes and pride of life—is not from the Father but is from the world."
>
> 1 John 2:15-16 ESV

I have a vision problem. I am very near-sighted. Ever since I was nine years old, if something is a few inches beyond the edge of my nose, it becomes very blurred and fuzzy. I lose details and I cannot see letters. I sometimes try to squint to be able to see better, but it usually doesn't help. The correction for my problem is obvious; I need glasses.

Since the third grade, I have had to make yearly trips to the optician. The optician takes the prescription I bring with me and he makes a pair of glasses to fix my focus. He crafts a pair of glasses that uses refraction to make my vision clear. Refraction is the bending of light so that things come into focus at the right point in my eye so the brain can see the image clearly. The optician must get this point of focus correct, or I still will not be able to see. And the really good opticians also help me pick out a pair of glasses that complement my face. After all, only some of us get the privilege to accessorize our faces with fantastic glassware.

In the passage today, God addresses focus. He tells us we can focus on the world, or we can focus on Him. Because the two are polar opposites, trying to see both at the same time will make our vision blurred and fuzzy.

We need the spiritual glasses of discernment to make sure we are seeing clearly. We need to take regular trips to the spiritual office of vision (prayer) to be sure we are focused on the right things. We need to spend time in God's Optical Room, reading His Word, and allowing Him to set our focus with the correct refraction of His light. We need to take time to confess our lack of focus to Him and to allow the Spirit of God to clear our vision. Only then will we see what is truly important in this life. We will see the details—the needs of others and the service God wants to administer through us— and we will be able to focus our energies in the right directions. And by abiding in His love, He will accessorize our faces with beautiful smiles and true joy—an added bonus for the time we take to wear His glasses and keep His focus.

Thought-provoker:

Are we visiting God's optical office and getting our focus from Him, or are we squinting through the world's lenses of greed and lust? Where does our focus need to change today?

Lord, we need You to focus our eyes on the right things, both physically and spiritually. Give us the spiritual vision we need, and help us not to be satisfied with worldly, blurry vision. In Jesus' name, Amen.

Notes/Insights:

The Painter

> "And after he had dismissed the crowds, he went up on the mountain by himself to pray. When evening came, he was there alone."
>
> Matthew 14:23 ESV

If you ask anyone who needs a painter in our circle of friends, Shay's name quickly comes up. Shay is an exceptional painter who not only has a steady hand and great eye, but also knows every trick and tip there is to make a paint project move along. Shay has a great instinct when it comes to colors and a good eye for bringing out architectural features. He can finish a room in half the time it takes others, and I envy his ability to paint without having to tape. Shay's hand is so steady, he can paint a straight line without a straight edge and I do not think I've ever heard of a drip of unwanted paint being left behind on a project he has done.

I was talking to Shay recently about helping me with a renovation project, and he confessed this to me: Shay does not like to paint. I thought he was joking at first, but he looked at me seriously and said, "Painting is a lonely job, and I like to be around people." Shay loves the part of designing and selling a project, but when it comes to the actual time spent painting, alone, he struggles. He likes conversation while he works, and it is tough to talk to a brush.

I think we all struggle with loneliness—even those of us who prefer to have alone time. It is in those times, however, that we need to be like Shay. When I asked him if he planned to quit painting, he said, "No, because I know I have a talent, but that doesn't mean I won't talk to myself while I am doing it." I appreciate his honesty, and yet, Jesus gave us the example of what to do when we are alone. Jesus found Himself alone on a mountain after having spent hours and hours with crowds of people. He had met needs, He had broadened His ministry, and now He was alone.

There on that mountain, He prayed. God Himself prayed. He had the benefit of knowing all, and yet He prayed. When He found Himself alone, He prayed. The God of the universe left us an example of what to do with loneliness; we realize we are never alone and talk to the One who is always with us.

Shay has started talking to God while he paints. He is realizing that being alone does not mean the same as being lonely, and he has learned to talk to the One who is always listening—even when there is a paintbrush in the hand of the one who is talking.

Thought-provoker:

How do we handle our loneliness? Are we talking to the One who is always with us, or are we overwhelmed by the feeling?

Lord, thank You that we are never alone, and prayer is a gift from You to fill the loneliness. Help us to take the time to pray, and to do it more often. In Jesus' name, Amen.

Notes/Insights:

The Pediatrician

> "Beloved, I pray that all may go well with you and that you may be in good health, as it goes well with your soul. For I rejoiced greatly when the brothers came and testified to your truth, as indeed you are walking in the truth. I have no greater joy than to hear that my children are walking in the truth."
>
> 3 John 1:2-4 ESV

Our children are older now, but we have had a great relationship with their pediatrician through the years. One of my first concerns when we moved to Tennessee was to find a pediatrician for our young family. With two energetic, young boys at the time, I wanted someone who would tell me the truth about their physical conditions, but also understood the energy and enthusiasm that came with being active and inquisitive little boys. Introducing our daughter to the family a short time later, I needed someone who understood the differences between the boys and a girl, and someone who was willing to give advice and direction about health issues and childhood development.

Dr. Kay was that person. She saw our family for the normal childhood visits and she was always happy to see our children healthy and growing. She was there for the difficult moments too. She sat in the chair next to me and explained what MRSA was and what we needed to do to treat it when our middle son got an infection from exploring, and getting cut, in the woods. She spent time explaining medications that our oldest had to be on after a seven-day stint in the hospital with a serious viral infection. She respected our belief in miracles and prayer and she rejoiced with us when the medications were no longer necessary.

What endeared me most to Dr. Kay, though, was when she announced she was retiring. She came in to see us one last time and told us that she was so happy she had the opportunity to help us to be in good health. She was glad she had been there as our pediatrician for those many years. She had been honest with us through the years, we had taken her advice and our children were, in essence, walking in the truth she had shared with us. She was happy for our good health. She rejoiced with us.

As we walk through life, we need to be happy for those whom God has allowed us to help—those with whom we have shared His truth. We are supposed to equip them and help them find the truth, and there is no greater joy than to know they are walking in it. Just as Dr. Kay was happy for our good health—we need to be happy for those whose healthy spiritual lives are credit to God's good will. Rejoice with them and celebrate.

Thought-provoker:

Are we looking for opportunities to celebrate the spiritual health of others around us? How can we encourage them to keep going today?

Father, rejoicing is a part of growing. Please show us the ones around us who need us to rejoice with them today and let's make a celebration! In Jesus' name, Amen.

Notes/Insights:

The Pedicurist

> "But God has so composed the body, giving greater honor to the part that lacked it, that there may be no division in the body, but that the members may have the same care for one another."
>
> I Corinthians 12:24b-25 ESV

Pedicurist. I love that word. It's such a fancy term for the person who makes my toes pretty. You see, I have small feet, and short toes to go along with them. I wear boots around the horses to protect my feet, and I wear sneakers a lot to support my arches. All of this is well and good—during the cooler months when everyone is wearing close-toed shoes. But then, spring and summer come along and my feet long to be seen in sandals or flip-flops. The callouses, the chipped pinky nail, and the heel marks, do not make my feet pretty—honestly, they look pretty rough. So, I make the appointment and I go see the pedicurist.

She soaks, scrubs and moisturizes my tough feet. She fills a soaker tub with warm sudsy water and turns on the massager as she gently dips my feet for a soak. She scrubs away the rough callouses and she pumices away the heel marks. She shapes the nails and displays her artistic abilities as she paints pretty flower petals on my big toes. When she is finished, my feet are ready and my toenails have become works of art just waiting to be displayed through the toes of my new spring shoes. Now, my feet look just as pretty as my hairdo and makeup on a Sunday morning. A trip to the pedicurist nurtures and cares for my feet the way a facial does for my cheekbones and a highlight does for my hair.

In the body of Christ, some of us are gifted as pedicurists. We see the potential in others that have been left to themselves, or have faced the harsh boots of life. They have marks, scars, or maybe they just feel rough and un-pretty in the pew. Spiritual pedicurists have the ability to gently come alongside—they help those rough individuals soak in the tub of God's forgiveness, to scrub away the guilt of the past and help paint a new future for the one who has felt unloved for so long.

They care for those who are less confident, and they help set them free to serve in the beautiful acceptance found in God's love. And many times, these rough individuals become the feet—the ones who are wiling to go, or the foundation that stands—all because a pedicurist came along and made them feel worthy and beautiful in the body of Christ.

Thought-provoker:

Are we caring for the rough individuals around us? If not, how can we reach out to show them spiritual pedicurist-care today?

Lord, thank You for the pedicurists who have the artistic ability to see potential and to bring out beauty in Your body. Help each of us to care for one another, whether we see a face or a foot, help us to love. In Jesus' name, Amen.

Notes/Insights:

The Photographer

"Teach the older men to exercise self-control, to be worthy of respect, and to live wisely. They must have sound faith and be filled with love and patience."

Titus 2:2 NLT

Almost everyone thinks they can use a camera; after all, social media is full of amateur pictures of everything from pets, to friends, to dinner plates. Cameras have become part of everyday life—they are even included in mobile devices. And while we use cameras to capture moments, sometimes the pictures can be very out of focus.

A professional photographer, on the other hand, can capture memories. Because he or she has been trained, they know what to look for, what to ignore and what is the most important focus in each picture. His eye is trained to look for the expression, or her lens is focused to catch the mood as well as the light. And, I am told, the longer a photographer works at the profession, the better focus he or she is able to find.

A friend of mine is a professional photographer, so I asked him how he determines what to shoot. His answer: "I focus on what is important at that moment and I ignore the rest." If he is shooting a basketball game, he focuses on the players. If it is senior portraits, he focuses on the face. If it is an outdoor family gathering, he includes the setting as he catches the candid shots of familial interaction. He has trained himself to know what to look for, where his focus should be, and he can filter out the things that just do not matter when the picture is developed.

Paul admonishes Titus to teach focus. In the passage today, the older men are to focus on character traits. There is not one mention of job success or wealth, but the focus is on their sound faith, self-control, wisdom, love and patience. To focus on these, they needed to ignore the urgencies of their day and times. They had to be thoughtful and careful as they walked through their life journeys. Their focus was to be on attributes, not attitudes. Their self-control would help avoid the pitfalls of pride and addiction. Love and faith would keep them grounded and wisdom and patience would keep them from rash decisions.

So, where is our focus? What do we deem important, where do we spend our efforts and energies? A photographer learns what to ignore because he or she wants the pictures to be memorable and pleasant for others to see. Our lives need to be focused on the important. As we allow God to shape our character, the other aspects of our lives will fall into place and the picture will be pleasant to us, and for others to enjoy.

Thought-provoker:
Where is the lens of focus in our lives today? Are we focused on the important or the urgent?

Father, thank You for Your Word that shows us what is important. Help us focus on attributes that please You so our life picture will be a pleasant one. In Jesus' name, Amen.

Notes/Insights:

The Pilot

"He leads the humble in what is right, and teaches the humble his way. All the paths of the Lord are steadfast love and faithfulness, for those who keep his covenant and his testimonies."

Psalm 25:9-10 ESV

There is an Air Show near our home every summer. As preparations are made, planes of all shapes and sizes pass over our home, headed to the airport. Massive C 130S, as well as Pipers, Cubs and bi-wings make their way to the airport for the grand event. I love to see the planes go by, hear their massive engines, or the hum of the smaller ones, and watch the planes as they gradually descend to the airstrip. What I am thankful for is that I am not in those planes. You see, I am not a huge fan of being that high up in the air, let alone with a pilot I have never met.

Our son, however, is studying to be a pilot. Because of this, we have come to know several pilots. Knowing them—knowing their names, their families, their credentials, has all made it easier for me to trust them as pilots. I still do not understand what they do, and I only have a basic understanding of flight mechanics and aerodynamics, but I can take a seat on one of those planes knowing the pilot knows me and has no intention of harming me, or my family, in any way. Because I have spent time getting to know them, it makes trusting them easier.

And, I am waiting for the day our son gets his license. I have promised him that I will go up with him and do my best to relax and enjoy the flight. Why can I make such a promise despite my fear of heights? Because I know him so very well; I have watched him grow into a fine young man and have seen the many hours of practice and study he has put into his flight program. So, when that day comes, I will enter that bird with confidence in the one I know is capable to fly that plane.

When we know the pilot, life is easier. When we get to know God Himself—the greatest Life Pilot of all time, we can have full confidence that He knows where the plane is going and how it is going to get there. The ride might be a little turbulent at times, but the Pilot will never lose control of the plane, and He will never take us into a storm that is not a part of His plan. Trust Him and get on the plane—His will for our lives. We will not understand every part of the mechanics or the dynamics of the journey, but we can trust the Pilot who knows all about it.

Thought-provoker:

Are we still standing on the ground, or are we trusting the Life Pilot and getting on His plane?

Father, when we do not understand the journey, please help us to trust You, the Pilot. In Jesus' name, Amen.

Notes/Insights:

The Plumber

"If we live in the Spirit, let us also walk in the Spirit."
Galatians 5:25 NKJV

It all started with a leaky showerhead. The constant dripping was wasting water and getting on our nerves, so we looked into fixing it ourselves. My husband is good with tools and fixing this problem was within his realm of skills, until we hit a snag. What should have been an easy replacement became a major home repair when I torqued the pipe instead of turning the joint. I broke the pipe in the wall, and when we turned the water back on in the house, it spewed out from the wall and all over the bathroom. We quickly shut it down and called a plumber.

The plumber cut a two-foot hole in the wall of the living room to reach the pipe. He was kind as he explained what I had done and gave my husband a grin as he explained my days with plumbing tools were over. What should have been an easy replacement had now become a major repair, and I had to spend the next weekend repainting the living room after the hole was fixed because we couldn't find the matching paint.

The plumber understood the power and energy of the water flowing in the pipes. He knew how to apply heat to bend the pipes and where to connect the joints so water flowed in the right direction at the right pressure. He also had the expertise to fix the leak in our showerhead unit and make the dripping stop.

The Holy Spirit understands the power and energy that flows through the house of God—the church. He knows how to apply heat to strengthen the pipes, the individuals of the church, through which that power flows, and He knows how to connect the pipes together so the power flows in the right direction. If the church energy had no leading and direction, it would make a major mess. Through the leading of the Holy Spirit, it has just the right impact to change the world around us.

And the dripping that disgruntles some of the church members? That is the drip of imperfection that happens because, sometimes, the pipes are not what they should be. The Holy Spirit is much better at fixing minor repairs in the church body than we are—we usually make a major mess of it. Instead of trying to fix it ourselves—ask the heavenly Plumber to come and do it.

Thought-provoker:

Are we following the leading of the Holy Spirit so the church energy and power can flow as it should, or are we trying to make the repairs ourselves and making a mess of things?

Father, thank You for the Spirit's leading and how He knows how to connect us to allow the church to have a greater impact for Your glory. Help us to leave the repairs in other's lives to Him and not take on something that isn't ours to do. Flow through us today and change the world around us. In Jesus' name, Amen.

Notes/Insights:

The Postal Worker

"And he said, 'Yes, it was written long ago that the Messiah would suffer and die and rise from the dead on the third day. It was also written that this message would be proclaimed in the authority of his name to all the nations, beginning in Jerusalem: "There is forgiveness of sins for all who repent." You are witnesses of all these things.'"

Luke 24:46-48 NLT

Diane works for the United States Postal Service. She is a good friend of mine, so I asked her about what she does. Each morning, she goes to the terminal, and finds the mail that has been designated for her route. She loads her truck with the letters, packages and other items she is to deliver, and then she starts her route.

Every day, she stops at the same mailboxes and delivers the messages sent to those individuals. Diane doesn't' write the message or box the packages, she simply delivers them to the intended recipients. It takes her all day—sometimes past dark, especially during the holiday season, to get all the messages delivered, but she does not stop until she finishes the route. Then, she goes back to the terminal and parks her truck, and goes home to rest until the next day to start the route again.

We have been given a message to take. We didn't write the message; we are just to deliver it. Just like Diane, God has specific people for each of us to reach—a route that He has designed for us to cover. Each morning, we should meet with Him in prayer and ask Him for the blessings He wants to deliver, whether they are the letters of the Gospel, a package of encouragement or a special surprise He has planned. We need to pack our hearts with His strength and readiness, as we get ready to run the route for that day.

Diane doesn't pack her truck for the whole week—the letters and packages wouldn't fit. She takes one day at a time, just as we need to go to God each day and ask what His plan is for our route.

Diane also doesn't get to choose to whom she delivers the messages. The route has been chosen for her by her supervisors and she doesn't get to say, "I don't like the way that house looks so I am not going to deliver the mail there today." Sometimes, God asks us to deliver His message to others that do not look right, or may seem very different from us. Deliver the message anyway—it's part of the route He has for us.

When it gets busy, keep doing the route you have been given. I love how God gives us the holidays as an "extra" opportunity to tell others about Him. Don't get discouraged, even when it takes all day to finish your route. And when the day is done, go park your truck in the terminal of praise and thanksgiving, and rest, because we will have another message to deliver in the morning.

Thought-provoker:

To whom are we supposed to deliver the message today?

Lord, thank You for the wonderful messages and blessings You give us the privilege to deliver. Help us be faithful to deliver on the route You have given us. In Jesus' name, Amen.

Notes/Insights:

The Preschool Teacher

> "See that you do not despise one of these little ones. For I tell you that in heaven their angels always see the face of my Father who is in heaven."
>
> Matthew 18:10 ESV

A friend of mine comes from a line of schoolteachers. Several of her siblings are educators at different levels, but she fell in love with the little ones. She is a preschool teacher and she is passionate about her job. She makes personalized items for each child in her class every year and she makes each child feel special as they "grow up" and get ready for the transition to a traditional kindergarten school setting.

Mrs. K. prepares her class with several goals in mind. She wants each one of them to be able to read when they leave her class. She wants them to be able to count, write their names and addresses and be able to recite songs and verses that will help them remember things for the following year. She also teaches them to use scissors and glue constructively, sharpen their own pencils and learn hallway manners. Each one of these goals is designed to help her students be ready and confident for the next steps in their elementary schooling and she wraps each child in respect as she works with them individually, or in groups. Unkind words and bullish behavior are not allowed in her classroom. Each child is unique and gifted, and they are to be treated as such.

At the end of each year, Mrs. K has a graduation ceremony. This program is an opportunity for parents to see how much their children have learned and see their children's unique talents displayed. Mrs. K gives each child a certificate that rewards him or her for a unique characteristic. I had to laugh one day last year when Mrs. K shared she had a class of almost all boys, and she was running out of positive, creative "boy" certificate ideas! Mrs. K wants each child to see the gifts and abilities they have, and she wants them to see their uniqueness in the body of Christ.

Just like Mrs. K, we need to be careful to see the good in others, especially little ones who are so influenced by our perceptions of them. We need to show each one of them respect, and show them we believe in their ability to make a difference. Sometimes, it takes creativity to find those words of affirmation, but it is so crucial that we do. Since angels are watching over these little ones, we know God sees their potential and their talents. We do well to watch over them too, and make sure they have the opportunities to become all He has planned.

Thought-provoker:

Are we despising or watching over the little ones entrusted in our circles of influence? What do we need to say to help them blossom and grow?

Lord, thank You for the preschool teachers who have the passion and ability to invest in the lives of little ones. Help us to find the encouraging, positive, creative things to say to them so they grow up to be all they should be. In Jesus' name, Amen.

Notes/Insights:

The Professional Organizer

> "We were buried therefore with him by baptism into death, in order that, just as Christ was raised from the dead by the glory of the Father, we too might walk in newness of life."
>
> Roman 6:4 ESV

I think I have found the "dream job" I want to do when I grow up. You know, when the kids are grown, the nest is empty and I have time to venture into another new profession. I want to be a Professional Organizer. A friend of mine is one, and people actually pay her for the organizational, de-cluttering, bring-peace-to-chaos skills that come so naturally to her. She is called upon to enter the chaotic offices, closets, and even entire homes of clients who have no idea how to simplify their systems and control the stuff that enters their domains. She sorts, confronts and masters clutter. She teaches them to write down their scheduled appointments and to keep them. She works with her clients to teach them a new way to live; a way that includes peace, progress, and hopefully—prosperity.

Jesus is the Master Professional Organizer. In His Word, He teaches us the skills we need to walk in "newness of life." He shows us how to live differently than the chaotic systems of the world, and He gives us the abilities we need to live uniquely—peacefully—in these difficult times. He recorded the timeless aspects of walking in the Spirit and not according to the chaotic desires of our natures (Galatians 5:16). He shows us how to make progress for the Heavenly Kingdom (Matthew 6:33; Ephesians 2) and He shows us how to prosper as children of God (John 15).

As we sort through the clutter of life, we have choices to make—as do the clients who hire my friend. She can set up new filing systems, she can show them how to keep a calendar of current activities and she can teach them how to track finances, but it is their choice whether or not they will live in this new way she shows them. They must use the principles she shares, and they have to adjust their way of thinking to less chaos and more order.

Jesus has already made it clear how He wants us to walk, He doesn't want confusion and chaos, His ways are clear, orderly and loving. Yet, we must choose to accept this new way of living and decide to change. And He is willing to walk through the process with us every step of the way.

Thought-provoker:

Are we living in the clarity and order of the loving ways of Christ, or are we choosing to live in the world's chaos and clutter? What one step does He ask of us today to move toward the newness of life He has for us?

Father, thank You that our lives can be organized around Your Word and Your principles so the newness of life shines through! Today, help us move toward the life of peace and progress You have for us and away from the world's chaos and confusion. Help us to live in the clarity of Your Word today. In Jesus' name, Amen.

Notes/Insights:

The Publisher

> "So neither he who plants nor he who waters is anything, but only God who gives the growth."
>
> I Corinthians 3:7 ESV

One of the important aspects of being an author is having a great publisher. Publishers are essential to the writing process because they are the ones who send the message of the writings or book into the market for others to see, read and purchase. Without a publisher, an author's writings are private doodlings on paper stuffed away in a drawer or a closet. An author's work is simply a private journal entry or an unknown work of art if it is not published for others to read.

Publishers have many responsibilities. They must acquire the rights to publish a work. This is both getting permission from the author to tell the story and making sure the story is appropriate to tell. They also have to plan, edit and design the manuscript. The publisher has to help the author say things clearly and sometimes that is a rough conversation because authors are particular about what they have said. The author put the words down, but it's the publisher who makes them look good. The publisher then takes on the responsibility of getting the book printed and sending it to the market. None of what the author has done matters if the book doesn't get into readers' hands.

The work of a publisher reflects the work of God in the life of a believer. We are all storytellers—our life stories are supposed to be shared to help others find Jesus. The publisher, though, determines how to present that story and where it needs to be published. What He needs from us is permission to tell our story and then our willingness to allow Him to mold it into a work of art. Those regrets we have—allow Him to make a chapter about new beginnings. Those glory moments—let Him temper them to show His glory, not ours. And those moments when we think we have utterly failed—He specializes in resurrection stories.

By allowing God to publish our stories, by giving Him permission to use the pieces of our lives as glimpses into His story, and by allowing Him to decide who needs to hear it, we give ourselves the best opportunity to impact the lives of others for the kingdom. Give Him permission to tell what others need to hear. Work willingly with Him as He rewrites those chapters of regrets and failures into faith adventures and hope for others. Allow God to publish your story.

Thought-provoker:

Have we given God permission to publish our story, to plan, design and determine the best version of us to share with others, or are we holding back? Where do we need to allow God to manage the rewrite today?

Father, thank You for being the One Who decides what our story should be. Help us to be willing to let You tell and publish it to whomever You see fit today. In Jesus' name, Amen.

Notes/Insights:

The Recycler

"By the sweat of your face you shall eat bread, till you return to the ground, for out of it you were taken; for you are dust, and to dust you shall return."

Genesis 3:19 ESV

There is a gentleman in our community who is very passionate about recycling. He owns a recycling center and he collects many different things—metals, batteries, aluminum, plastics, the list goes on. He has piles of the different materials in his lot and you simply add to his piles by driving up and dumping your addition to the materials. Then, you drive away and can forget about it. Every few days, the gentleman loads up his truck with one of the piles and he takes the materials to the various sites for recycling. He takes plastics to be melted down and reused; tires are taken to the grinder to be turned into playground bedding, and cardboards are taken to the factory to be rebound and reformed. Other materials are loaded and taken to their appropriate centers for reuse.

God is the ultimate recycler. Trees grow from dirt. The tree flourishes and nourishes from nutrients in the dirt, then it grows old, dies and falls back to the earth and becomes the elements of dirt again, from which another tree can grow. Plants grow, produce seeds and then die and the seeds become plants again. Water rains all the earth, runs into creeks, rivers and lakes; it evaporates and joins the clouds and becomes rain again. All of this is part of God's design. His great plan of recycling.

The two things God does not recycle are time and our souls. There is no replacement for any of us—we are each one-of-a-kind. God's love for us is so immense that He made each of us with one individual soul. We do not share our souls—we each have our own. Our bodies will live, grow, die and decompose, as part of His design, but our souls will not. God places such value on each of us that we cannot be recycled or reused, and neither can the time He has given us. Once a day passes, we cannot get it back. We cannot pull up to the time factory and recycle our hours and minutes. Once they are gone, they cannot be replaced.

Because of the value God has placed on our souls and time, so valuable they cannot be recycled, we need to treasure both. Recycle what you can; treasure what you cannot. We need to choose where our souls will spend eternity, and we need to choose how we spend our moments. Both are precious to God, and so they should be to us as well. Choose wisely.

Thought-provoker:

Are we treating our souls like recycling, or are we treasuring them as the unique creations God intended? Have we settled the question of where our souls will spend eternity and are we choosing wisely for the moments we are given?

Lord, thank You for the treasures of souls and time. Help us to choose wisely when it comes to both of them. In Jesus' name, Amen.

Notes/Insights:

The Salesman

> "Walk in wisdom toward them that are without, redeeming the time. Let your speech be always with grace, seasoned with salt, that ye may know how ye ought to answer every man."
> Colossians 4:5-6 KJV

My husband had a sneaky secret…shortly after we moved to our new house; he would sometimes leave for a couple of hours. He was meeting with someone—he was meeting with someone who knew about tractors. He had several meetings with the tractor guy before I found out that the meetings were in preparation for the purchase of our newest farm addition. Buying a tractor is not an impulse-purchase. It took time to find out all the ins and outs of the different models, what features we needed on our new property, what different supplements we would need to add, and other information like horsepower and torque ratio.

The tractor salesman is an honest, straight-talking guy. He was patient, answered a lot of questions, and asked questions to help John in the knowledge process. He got to know my husband, knew his name, his interests, and yes, his phone number too. When the day came that the tractor we needed had come onto the lot, we got a phone call, and the purchase was made. The relationship didn't stop there, though. There were further conversations about delivery and warranty, and follow-up phone calls to be sure we were satisfied, happy, with our purchase.

Instead of "salesman" for his job title, I prefer to call him the tractor relationship guy. The first day John met him, he made an impression. He was knowledgeable, but not pushy, and he was willing to give John time and space until he was ready to make a decision. As the meetings continued, he showed interest in what we were trying to accomplish, he wanted to assist us with knowledge and help us to find exactly what we were looking for. When the day came to make our purchase, he was happy for us and joined in the excitement as the tractor came to our home.

We, as believers, are salesman for the Gospel. We could be demanding and push people to make decisions about accepting the salvation that is offered, but a better approach is to build relationships with them. We take the time to get to know them, and we offer the opportunity to accept God's grace as the Lord gives us the opportunity. We are patient as they ask questions, we help them to gain more knowledge of God, and we are wiling to spend time with them. And it pays off. When they willingly accept the offer of saving grace, they ask us to join in the happiness and excitement of that decision. We get to celebrate their decision with them and we then have the opportunity to follow up and continue the relationship with a new brother or sister in Christ.

Thought-provoker:

Are you pushy or patient when dealing with those who do not know Christ? Are you building relationships with others to help them find Jesus?

Lord, please help us to build relationships with others and to share You with others instead of trying to sell them salvation. Help us to say the right things at the right time. In Jesus' Name, Amen.

Notes/Insights:

The Wood Cutter

"Be diligent to present yourself approved to God, a worker who does not need to be ashamed, rightly dividing the word of truth."
2 Timothy 2:15 NKJV

I know that there are professionals who cut down trees, chop wood, and split logs for a living. They do a fantastic job of clearing land, managing harvest maps, and rotating the cutting sites so that new trees have time to grow and mature. I confess that I am not one of them. I have, however, started to split wood because we have a wood-burning fireplace, and several trees have fallen on our property. My husband and sons use chainsaws to chop the trees into manageable pieces, then we stack them by the barn, and we get some much-needed exercise as they work, and I get practice splitting the wood.

Another confession—I am not the greatest wood-cutter. Not even close. Sometimes, it takes me several swings of the axe before I make even a dent in the end of the wood. On occasion, though, I split a piece with one swing. Usually, it is a smaller width and a dry piece, but I get it nonetheless. My husband, however, can split massive pieces with one or two strokes. You see, he is a foot taller than me and he has the ability to swing the axe 360 degrees. I have to keep the axe in front of me because when I try to swing 360 degrees, it catches the ground on the upswing.

But, I keep at it. Each time I swing, my muscles get stronger. I've watched other "vertically-challenged" individuals split wood, and I am learning from their technique. I am getting better with each session of practice.

Bible study is like woodcutting. Some people, through experience and skill, have massive skills. They split difficult truths into simpler parts with just one or two sessions of study. My friend Ruth is like that. Her Bible study skills are like a chain saw, cutting through false ideas from our culture and applying truths in everyday situations. But, for those of us who are not the best at it, we get better as we keep trying. It may take us longer to grasp an idea or a concept about God, but we don't stop until the log splits and we see the treasure in His Word. We learn from others, we try again and again, and we find methods of study that work for us. We allow the Holy Spirit to teach us and we get spiritually stronger in the process. So, go get your study axe and swing it again—doesn't matter how many swings it takes, it is that you keep swinging that truly matters.

Thought-provoker:

Are you being intentional about your Bible study, even if it feels clumsy or awkward for now? What swings are working for you as you study truths from God's Word?

Lord, help us to keep swinging when it comes to digging into the truths of Your Word. Please do not let us get lazy when it comes to spiritual exercise, and show us the best ways You have planned for us to learn from Your Word. In Jesus' Name, Amen.

Notes/Insights:

The Sanitation Worker

> "For his unfailing love toward those who fear him is as great as the height of the heavens above the earth. He has removed our sins as far from us as the east is from the west."
> Psalm 103:11-12 NLT

Well, it happened. One of the hottest days of the summer, the kind where eggs would fry on cement and butter would melt on the counter, and I had to run errands. It would not have been too bad, but as I came around a deep corner, there it was in front of me. The garbage truck, fully loaded, was stopping at each driveway on the main road to pick up more garbage. While I am grateful for their sanitation services, I was not grateful at the moment when I saw them at work. It was hot, the garbage smelled, and I was stuck behind them. Every driveway. I kept my distance, but there was no way to avoid the smell. As they turned into a subdivision about a half-mile later, I finally exhaled and drove past before I took in another breath. Grateful to have distance between them and me, I finally started to breathe normally again and relax.

I wonder if our sin smells like that garbage to God. As I sat behind that truck, I could barely breathe. The smell was nauseating and my body rebelled against the intake of such odor. I coughed if I breathed too deeply and I could not wait to be free from the stench. What if God feels that way about our stinky sin? What if He cannot stand the stench of our selfishness or the nauseating odor of our pride? If I could not stand the few moments behind the sanitation truck, how could God stand the constant smell of my sinfulness?

Then, it struck me. God is the garbage truck driver. Our sin smells so bad to Him that He had to put redemption in place to keep it from separating us from Him. He is willing to drive the truck of redemption, so that our sins can be removed, and we can have a sweet relationship with Him once again.

I have never been able to look at a sanitation truck in disgust since. That driver, those workers, who put up with that smell and the garbage itself, so that we can live in a clean environment, represent God's willingness to take our sin from us. They do it for a paycheck and the purpose of their job; God does it because of His great love for us. He is willing to do what we cannot—He takes our sins away. He is willing to drive that truck of redemption; are we willing to accept His gift of grace?

Thought-provoker:

Are we ready for a relationship that is sweet and savory with the God who loves us? Do we appreciate His sacrifice to save our souls and remove our sin?

Father, thank You for the redemption You provided to take our sin from us. Help us live in the sweetness of a gracious relationship with You today. In Jesus' name, Amen.

Notes/Insights:

The Server

"Oh, taste and see that the Lord is good! Blessed is the man who takes refuge in him!"

Psalm 34:8 ESV

Being a waitress, server, or any other form of food delivery personnel is a field of formidable obstacles. Learning the computer system, knowing the menu, pricing, specials and drink options is just the beginning. There is also the table setting, the restocking of condiments and the kitchen route (yes, there is a flow of traffic in a kitchen so servers are not running into each other). On top of all of this, they must learn good customer service skills and how to handle questions and spills. And here this poor girl was dealing with me. I had never been to the restaurant before and I was having a hard time deciphering what I could eat from the menu. With food allergies, one always must be careful when trying new dishes.

This young lady, however, was exceptional at her job. Not only was she able to tell me the ingredients in certain menu items, but she also had opinions and suggestions. I was not annoyed in the least by her suggestions and opinions—because she had based both on her experience. She had tried every menu item at some point in the past and she knew whether each item was spicy, bland, greasy, gutsy or bold. Because of her willingness to share information based on her own experience, I trusted her judgment and I was able to choose a delicious dish and enjoy the meal.

The Lord is not a dish at a restaurant, but He does tell us to "taste and see." He wants us to experience His grace, goodness, mercy, holiness and justice. He wants us to have a firsthand knowledge of courage in the face of adversity that comes straight from His heart to us, of peace in the midst of testing and anxiety, and of strength that comes from His might as we struggle with our human frailties.

When we have truly experienced the highs and the lows of life and He has sustained us and restored our joy, then we can graciously lead others to the table and help them find the delicious dishes of grace and mercy that help in times of need. God wants us to be exceptional at our job of leading others to Him, so He gives us varied experiences that open doors of opportunity to credibly share how we find Him to be faithful and true. He wants us to have a working knowledge of the good things on His menu and be able to share our suggestions with others. When we do this well, God is honored and the dishes of salvation, mercy and grace are well received.

Thought-provoker:

What kind of servers are we as we dish up God's love and goodness to a scared and sinful world? What experiences make us exceptional servers today?

Lord, thank You for allowing us the privilege to share Your grace and goodness with others. Help us to use the dishes of experience we each have to recommend others come and taste and see just how good You are. In Jesus' name, Amen.

Notes/Insights:

The Soldier

"You therefore must endure hardship as a good soldier of Jesus Christ. No one engaged in warfare entangles himself with the affairs of this life, that he may please him who enlisted him as a soldier."
2 Timothy 2:3-4 ESV

My family has been blessed to have the privilege of enlisted personnel among our heritage. Grandparents, aunts and uncles, cousins and brothers have heeded the call to serve our country. All have served honorably and we are proud of each one of them. As a family, we have tried to be supportive during deployments—offering prayers of protection, sending love and encouragement through emails and letters and sending a piece of our hearts to war-torn places in packages and gifts.

One of our family members is currently serving as a Navy sailor and we know the feeling of missing his presence and humor at the holiday table. We have set a chair at the table to remind us he is a part of us, even when he's half a world away. The phone calls—hearing his voice and connecting for those few brief moments are treasures worth every penny of international rates.

Being a soldier is challenging; being a soldier's family is tough too. Sacrifices are made, separation occurs and hearts sometimes hurt.

But, the reunions are amazing! The holidays when we are together—to be able to sit at the table, enjoying each other's company, laughing at jokes, listening to stories. The sacrifices dim in the background as the love of family and the precious process of memory making takes center stage.

God asks us to endure hardship—the life of sacrifices—as good soldiers. He asks us to teach others by our example to bear up under the trials and carry the weight of those who mock our faith in Him. Being a soldier for the kingdom is challenging, and knowing this, God provided a family. He has given us a worldwide family of believers who pray for us as we deploy on our individual missions for the kingdom, encourage us, build us up and even send us resources and love as we serve. And what a family to reunite with when we get to come back and rest for a holiday. They join us at the table, listen to our stories, restore us with laughter and reenergize us with precious times of connection and memory making. I am so grateful God saw fit to make us all part of His soldier-family. Pray for those who are deployed and enjoy the moments around the family table.

Thought-provoker:

Are we supporting those who are deployed in heavenly ministry through prayers, encouragement and resources? Are we connecting, as the family of God should be?

Abba, thank You for the family You have provided for all of Your soldiers. Help us support, encourage and love each other as we serve in the missions You have given each of us. Please remind us to enjoy the times of restoration around the family table. In Jesus' name, Amen.

Notes/Insights:

The Song Writer

"He has put a new song in my mouth—praise to our God; Many will see it and fear, and will trust in the LORD."

Psalm 40:3 NKJV

Living near Nashville, we have met several people who are a part of the music industry. There are aspiring singers, audio technicians, managers and agents. There are also songwriters. One of our friends is a songwriter and I have talked with him on occasion about what makes a "hit." He believes a song has a good chance of being competitive in the market if it is written from a personal experience with emotion. Not out-of-control emotion, but feelings that convince the listener the song is worth hearing to the end. The song should tell a story, and the lyrics and the music need to work together to make a convincing piece. He blends the chords and melody to make a beautiful background to the story and he knits the story together so it makes sense.

I thought it would be fun to attempt to write a song. After all, I write stories and see illustrations everywhere, how hard could it be to write a song? After several hours of attempting, and only three measures of music and one clumsy verse, I humbly handed in my song-writing pen. It is much more difficult than most can picture. Trying to make the words fit into a rhythm that matches a set of tones; trying to tell a story in limited syllables and lines; and then trying to make it fit together so that the chorus can be repeated between verses—not to mention the music theory, pentameter and other aspects of the music itself—it was not fun. It was work. I found a new appreciation for our friend's skill and ability as he does this work on a daily basis. It is not as easy as it seems and there are many aspects to it that most people do not consider. The goal of a songwriter is to hear his song being sung by another.

God, the Master Song-writer, has written a song into each one of our lives. He has blended the perfect combination of experience and emotion—He makes each lyric and note fit together in a beautiful orchestration called our lives. He blends the chords of suffering and joy; He combines stories and themes through our lives and He makes the song make sense. He makes the song interesting and each one of our lives interesting and worth seeing to the end. He doesn't expect us to write the song, plan the meter, or pick the melody. He doesn't ask us to blend chords and write choruses. What does He ask of us? God wants us to sing the songs He has written for each one of us.

Thought-provoker:

Are you singing the song God has written for you? How will you let others hear your song today?

Lord, thank You for the song that You have written for each of us to sing. Help us to share our songs and share You as the Master Song-writer. In Jesus' Name, Amen.

Notes/Insights:

The Veteran

"Older men are to be level headed, worthy of respect, sensible, and sound in faith, love, and endurance."

Titus 2:2 HCSB

Ron is a quiet, reserved, older gentleman. He speaks softly and moves gently. He has a kind word for every person he meets. He talks in a steady rhythm, but not the kind that puts you to sleep. It's the kind of rhythm that makes you lean in to hear each word, and find yourself engaged in the story he is telling.

Ron is a veteran and a war hero, but you wouldn't know that by just passing him on the street. He doesn't wear his medals on his chest or wear his uniform to church. Ron could sit back and say that he has done his part, that it's his turn to rest now and allow others to do. But that's not Ron's way.

Ron has realized the next generation still needs him. They need him to share his story, the facts about what he saw, the battles he fought and the victories he won. He needs to tell them how to handle life when it becomes difficult, how to sludge through the mud of the jungle, march through the darkness and learn how to use their weapons well. Though Ron fought in physical wars, he has also engaged in the spiritual battles over lost souls, over wandering saints and rebellious prodigals.

He understands we still have enemies and the spiritual war is not over. Instead of sitting and watching, he is engaging and teaching. He softly, carefully, shares with younger men how to be the men of God for the next generation. His experiences and his integrity have made him worthy of respect. He shares the principles of endurance and his testimony of faith with love. He sensibly engages others in the battle as he comes alongside of them with encouragement and prayers.

When he shares his history, he points others to the endurance he has found in his relationship with Christ. He doesn't boast about his accomplishments; he focuses on God's power and protection in his life. Ron openly shares about struggles and pain he has endured and he encourages others to find the same source of strength he has found—in the everlasting love of Jesus Christ. The church needs its war heroes, like Ron, to share and to inspire the next generation of leaders and warriors so they will be ready to stand (Ephesians 6). Thankfully, Ron has not sat back, he is standing up and preparing those who are willing to engage the enemy and win the victory.

Thought-provoker:

Where can our veteran skills be engaged in the spiritual battle today? Are we encouraging and praying for others? Are we sitting back or standing up to help the next generation?

Father, thank You for those who have gone before and have learned how to fight the battle of faith well. Help us to listen and to learn from them and thank You for the victory we have in Jesus Christ. In His name, we fight on, Amen.

Notes/Insights:

The Weather Forecaster

"The heart of man plans his way, but the Lord establishes his steps."

Proverbs 16:9 ESV

I watch the weather forecasts with interest. I know no matter how hard they try, the forecasters will miss something, and that is okay, because they still get to keep on forecasting. I sometimes watch with personal amusement as they attempt to figure out a ten-day forecast. The weather station in our local area has a five-arm radar system that detects weather patterns from all directions. They have computer models and scientific equipment to determine where and when the fronts will move and they predict whether there is enough moisture in the atmosphere to cause storms. Even with all that equipment and planning, the weather patterns change at the last moment, a storm stalls out, or it comes in faster than expected.

But, every now and then, they get it right. Because of their training and trust in the scientific principles of weather, they can determine when dangerous storms are approaching and they are able to warn others to find safety and shelter. These moments make their job vital—the ability to warn others by seeing the dangers and making preparations.

Life is like the weather. We can plan for it and try to figure out the when and where of how things are going to happen. We can use planners, programs and applications to predict what our days will be like and how things should go. We try very hard to know what is coming next. It's good to plan, but it is also wise to realize that plans are just that—plans. They are not a sure-fire contract that guarantees how our days will turn out. James 4 tells us we do not know what a day will hold. He tells us to be sure we rely on the Lord's will when we make plans. That way, we aren't rattled when an unexpected storm comes or a dry spell up-ends our forecast.

But, we also have the principles of Scripture and the training God administers in our lives to be able to see certain storms and dangers on the horizon and to be able to warn others. God tells us to prepare for our futures by accepting His Son as our shelter from an eternity separated from Him. He tells us to be good stewards (1 Peter 4:10), to not trust in our worldly riches, to give generously from the rich blessings He gives us (1 Timothy 6:17-20) and to trust Him for the direction we need in our lives (Proverbs 3:5-6). By doing these things, we can find shelter from danger and help protect others—and that is why forecasting is important.

Thought-provoker:

How are we balancing planning for life events with trusting the Lord's will? Are we warning others of the dangers we can see?

Father, thank You for the principles in Your Word and the discernment You give us to enable us to see dangers, warn others and find our shelter in You. Make us good forecasters for Your kingdom today. In Jesus' name, Amen.

Notes/Insights:

The Staffing Personnel

"Being confident of this very thing, that He who has begun a good work in you will complete it until the day of Jesus Christ."
Philippians 1:6 NKJV

Staffing personnel want the right person for the right job. They want the right fit. They want someone to begin a good job and stick with it. Their job is to connect people with skills with companies needing those skills. They link open positions in companies with people who are willing and capable to fill those jobs. The staffing personnel administer aptitude tests to determine what skills and talents a worker has and what is a good fit for them. They spend time learning about the job positions and what companies are looking for when they are ready to hire. Staffing personnel assign workers to jobs that will hopefully become full-time employment and benefit both the worker and the company.

According to our passage, God is the staffing personnel of life jobs, and He is very good at what He does. As Creator, He knows very well what we each are designed to do. He knows our aptitudes, intellect, abilities, strengths and weaknesses. He determines what job is best for us and what is the best fit, and when we fill those positions, we are fulfilled. We find the benefits of being in a position that uses our talents and helps us to be a part of His great company, the heavenly kingdom.

God assigns different jobs to each one of us. Some of us are given abilities to work with our hands, to dream, to build, to create. Others are given skills to solve problems, to find solutions, to harness potential or make things grow. Still others are given the talents to teach others, to share ideas and to open doors of possibilities to others.

As we go about our work, we are to love those around us. Different as we may be, we are all part of His glorious plan; we are needed and we are here for a purpose. As we finish this devotional journey through the work of our lives, may we realize each of us has been given a gift in the work we do. We have been blessed as God has given each of us responsibilities and duties to fulfill on this earth as we interact and connect with others. Whatever the job you have been assigned to do, do it well, do it diligently and do it for His glory. Go enjoy your calling!

Thought-provoker:

As we come to the end of this devotional journey, my hope and prayer is that you have seen the blessings of work and the potential for connection with those who work in different fields. We have each been given a calling—let's work together for the kingdom and look forward to the day Jesus completes His work in us.

Father, thank You for the work You've given each of us to do. Help us go and be busy doing Your kingdom work in our everyday lives. In Jesus' name, Amen.

Notes/Insights:

About the Author

Tammy Chandler is a wife, mother, teacher, friend, author and public speaker. She accepted Christ as Savior when she was five years old, dedicated her life to full-time service as a teenager and has worked in various ministries for the past twenty years. She has a bachelor of education degree from Clearwater Christian College, and a master of education from Jones International University. After many years of using everyday objects to teach children and teenagers, God allowed her to write Devotions from Everyday Things (Westbow Press), its follow-up, More Devotions from Everyday Things, Devotions from Everyday Things: Horse and Farm Edition, and now Devotions from Everyday Jobs to include a larger audience.

When she is not writing, Tammy enjoys spending time with her husband, John, watching their sons play sports, going horseback riding with their daughter, or playing fetch with their dog, Ava. The Chandlers live in Tennessee.

Visit Tammy online at:

www.simplydevotions.wordpress.com

You might also enjoy these fine books from:

WordCrafts Press

More Devotions from Everyday Things
by Tammy Chandler

Devotions from Everyday Things
(Horse & Farm Edition)
by Tammy Chandler

Chewing the Daily Cud, Vol. 1 & 2
(Daily Ruminations on the Word of God)
by Rodney Boyd

Pondering(s)
by Wayne Berry

I Wish Someone Had Told Me
by Barbie Loflin

Illuminations
by Paula K. Parker & Tracy Sugg

www.wordcrafts.net

Made in the USA
Middletown, DE
30 March 2019